MARXISM *and* COMMUNISM

Essential Readings

STUDIES IN POLITICAL SCIENCE

RANDOM HOUSE   NEW YORK

MARXISM
and COMMUNISM
Essential Readings

Edited by ROBERT V. DANIELS
THE UNIVERSITY OF VERMONT

ACKNOWLEDGMENTS

I am indebted to the University of Vermont and the Rockefeller Foundation for support of my research work during the period when this project was in progress. I have been ably assisted in the preparation of the manuscript by Mrs. Katherine Marston and Mrs. Gertrude Parkhill.

R. V. D.

Contents

PART THREE • VARIETIES OF COMMUNISM

Introduction—Studying the Documents of Communism

The international political movement we know as "Communism" is inescapably of major significance in any approach to the study of human affairs—whether this be from the standpoint of the historian, the political scientist, the economist, the sociologist, or the philosopher. One of the dominant historical forces of the twentieth century, Communism is a leading political and economic alternative for the peoples of the world, as well as an elaborate philosophical system. Acquaintance with its history, goals, problems, and beliefs is essential for anyone who hopes to find his way about in the modern world.

A salutary trend in American teaching of the social sciences has been the recent turn toward the use of original and documentary sources in order to determine the actual character of the thinking and behavior of important individuals or movements. This approach is particularly necessary in the study of Communism, a movement in which theoretical texts and historical analogies serve to inspire, justify, or reflect political action. A comprehensive collection of excerpts from important writings in the history of the Communist movement is therefore a minimum requisite for the student who is beginning to examine the subject. This present brief volume of readings is presented to meet that need.

There are a number of drawbacks in many of the extant anthologies bearing on Communism; the present collection is designed to avoid them. Most collections of documents covering Communism are either too long or too specialized for the beginning student. This applies, for example, to my own *Documentary History of Communism* (New York, Vintage Books, 1962, 2 vols.), which begins with Lenin and is intended for the more advanced student in Russian history, comparative government, political philosophy and the like. On the other hand, the general anthologies prepared for survey courses in history and government are usually too limited in their coverage of Communism, and usually omit many of the most significant statements of Marxism and Communism. This selection of readings has been compiled in order to provide the student in the general course, or the general nonspecialist reader, with a sampling of materials that is brief enough to become part of a regular reading program, and yet both representative and comprehensive. Emphasis is placed on key writings often omitted from general anthologies, such as Marx's Introduction to the *Critique of Political Economy,* and his *Critique of the Gotha Program,* Lenin's *What is to Be Done?,* and Stalin's programmatic speeches of 1931. Furthermore, some important but usually neglected sources of Communist thinking are represented here—the Russian background of revolutionary socialism, as enunciated by Alexander Herzen; the early Russian Marxism of Plekhanov; the democratic "revision" of Marxism represented by the late writings of Engels and by Eduard Bernstein; finally, materials illustrating some of the various national approaches in today's debates over "polycentric" Communism.

Certain cautions should be voiced concerning the use of theoretical and programmatic texts in studying any movement, particularly Communism. The Communist movement purports to base itself on the scientific laws of historical development supposedly discovered by Marx. However, the beliefs of a movement are not necessarily in accord with its nature; if it were so, we would have to accept, for instance, the Communists' assertion that the Soviet Union is the world's "most democratic" country. The movement may not be fulfilling the place in its own theory which it ascribes to itself; as Trotsky hinted in his "New Course" letters of 1923, and in many later writings, the Soviet Union may not be a genuine example of the "dictatorship of the proletariat." It is also possible that the whole "scientific" theory of Marx and his followers may be wrong, in which case it becomes necessary to develop a new description of the actual Communist systems and an independent explanation of them. Such a task, naturally, is beyond the scope of the present introductory collection, but for my own essay in that direction the reader may consult *The*

Nature of Communism (New York, Vintage Books, 1963).

One important by-product of the study of Communism is the insight it affords into the general relationship between thought and action in human affairs. It is well known that people do not always say what they mean or do what they say. In reading Communist material, the perceptive reader is constantly reminded that theoretical statements do not always serve as guides to existing reality or to subsequent practice. Such statements, even if couched in universal terms, may often be responses to specific problems or events, and thus, lose much of their relevance later. They may even be contrived as propaganda or for political effect, especially when the spokesmen of theory possess dictatorial power. There has been, I believe, a growing divergence of practice from theory, and as a result a frequent reinterpretation of theory to attempt to make it fit reality, as the Communist movement has evolved from Marx through Lenin to Stalin and his successors. Now the same theory is being used as a weapon by the two great Communist governments in Moscow and Peking to berate each other for "deviation" and "treachery." Nevertheless, the pronouncements of top Communist spokesmen illustrate the emotions driving the leaders of the movement and the way in which they try to use their opportunities and solve their problems.

The desire for brevity in the present collection has made it impossible to illustrate all the important events, policies and ideas in the history of Communism. I hope the reader will consult the historical texts for the narrative picture, if he does not have the organized framework of a formal academic course. In this book the reader will find excerpts from these programmatic texts of Communism which are most important to know, because of the role they play as guidelines or as means of political justification. But the reader should look between the lines as well, in order to recognize not only the intellectual continuities in Communism, but also the profound evolution and variety in a movement that, paradoxically, represents itself as the undeviating application of a single philosophy.

PART ONE

MARXISM

The official doctrine of the Communist movement is Marxism-Leninism, the revolutionary philosophy of Karl Marx as modified and updated by V. I. Lenin. Marxism is the basic philosophical source from which Communism draws its terms and ideas, many of its assumptions, and its general style of thinking. This is not to say that Marxist doctrine has dictated everything the Communists have done or intended, or that Leninism has been the only possible way of developing Marxism. It is possible to envisage at least two alternative developments from the earliest statements—gradual and peaceful changes, as represented by the last two selections from Engels and Bernstein, in this chapter, and abrupt violent change as represented in the selections from Lenin's writings.

At the center of Marx's theory lies his prediction of a world-wide revolution by the proletariat—factory workers—and their creation of a new social order, termed "socialism" or "communism." In proposing such a goal, Marx was preceded by a number of early nineteenth-century theorists, the "Utopian Socialists"—notably the Frenchman St. Simon and the Welshman Owen. Other schemes for a communist society can be traced back to Thomas More (author of *Utopia*), and even to Plato and his *Republic*. What Marx did was to combine the ideal of socialism with newer currents of thought, particularly the German philosophy of historical evolution (Hegel) and the British study of economics (Adam Smith and Ricardo). The resulting synthesis sought to demonstrate that proletarian socialism or communism was the inevitable outcome of the economic development of capitalist society. This belief was destined to have more influence around the world than any other modern idea.

MARX and ENGELS: THE THEORY OF PROLETARIAN REVOLUTION

Karl Marx (1818-1883) and Friedrich Engels (1820-1895) began a life-long collaboration during the 1840's in France, after both had been forced to leave their native Germany as political exiles. The first widely known statement of their beliefs was The Manifesto of the Communist Party, *published in Paris just before the Revolution of 1848 broke out. Although, as Engels explains in his introduction to the 1888 translation of the Manifesto, some of its points had already become outdated, it is nonetheless justly regarded as the best summary of the Marxist theory of capitalist society and proletarian revolution. The selection that follows includes Parts I and II of the* Manifesto *in their entirety, and the concluding passages of Part IV; the omitted material is of little present-day interest.*

ENGELS' PREFACE TO THE 1888 ENGLISH TRANSLATION OF THE COMMUNIST MANIFESTO

The Manifesto was published as the platform of the "Communist League," a workingmen's association, first exclusively German, later on international, and, under the political conditions of the Continent before 1848, unavoidably a secret society. At a Congress of the League, held in London in November, 1847, Marx and Engels were commissioned to prepare for publication a complete theoretical and practical party program. Drawn up in German, in January, 1848, the manuscript was sent to the printer in London a few weeks before the French revolution of February 24th. A French translation was brought out in Paris, shortly before the insurrection of June, 1848. The first English translation, by Miss Helen Macfarlane, appeared in George Julian Harney's "Red Republican," London, 1850. A Danish and a Polish edition had also been published. . . .

From our joint preface to the German edition of 1872, I quote the following:

"However much the state of things may have altered

From Karl Marx and Friedrich Engels, *The Manifesto of the Communist Party* (Moscow, Foreign Languages Publishing House), pp. 17, 24-25, 46-90, 113-114.

during the last twenty-five years, the general principles laid
down in this Manifesto are, on the whole, as correct today
as ever. Here and there some detail might be improved.
The practical application of the principles will depend, as
the Manifesto itself states, everywhere and at all times, on
the historical conditions for the time being existing, and,
for that reason, no special stress is laid on the revolutionary
measures proposed at the end of Section II. That passage
would, in many respects, be very differently worded today.
In view of the gigantic strides of modern industry since
1848, and of the accompanying improved and extended
organization of the working class, in view of the practical
experience gained, first in the February Revolution, and
then, still more, in the Paris Commune, where the proletariat for the first time held political power for two whole
months, this program has in some details become antiquated. One thing especially was proved by the Commune,
viz., that 'the working class cannot simply lay hold of
the readymade State machinery, and wield it for its own
purposes.' "

THE MANIFESTO OF THE COMMUNIST PARTY

A specter is haunting Europe—the specter of Communism.
All the powers of old Europe have entered into a holy alliance to exorcise this specter: Pope and Czar, Metternich
and Guizot, French Radicals and German police-spies.

Where is the party in opposition that has not been de-
cried as Communistic by its opponents in power? Where
the Opposition that has not hurled back the branding reproach of Communism, against the more advanced opposition parties, as well as against its reactionary adversaries?

Two things result from this fact.

I. Communism is already acknowledged by all European
powers to be itself a power.

II. It is high time that Communists should openly, in the
face of the whole world, publish their views, their aims,
their tendencies, and meet this nursery tale of the specter
of Communism with a Manifesto of the party itself.

To this end, Communists of various nationalities have assembled in London, and sketched the following Manifesto, to be published in the English, French, German, Italian, Flemish and Danish languages.

I. BOURGEOIS AND PROLETARIANS

The history of all hitherto existing society is the history of class struggles.

Freeman and slave, patrician and plebeian, lord and serf, guildmaster and journeyman, in a word, oppressor and oppressed, stood in constant opposition to one another, carried on an uninterrupted, now hidden, now open fight, a fight that each time ended, either in a revolutionary reconstitution of society at large, or in the common ruin of the contending classes.

In the earlier epochs of history, we find almost everywhere a complicated arrangement of society into various orders, a manifold gradation of social rank. In ancient Rome we have patricians, knights, plebeians, slaves; in the Middle Ages, feudal lords, vassals, guildmasters, journeymen, apprentices, serfs; in almost all of these classes, again, subordinate gradations.

The modern bourgeois society that has sprouted from the ruins of feudal society has not done away with class antagonisms. It has but established new classes, new conditions of oppression, new forms of struggle in place of the old ones.

Our epoch, the epoch of the bourgeoisie, possesses, however, this distinctive feature: it has simplified the class antagonisms. Society as a whole is more and more splitting up into two great hostile camps, into two great classes directly facing each other: bourgeoisie and proletariat.

From the serfs of the Middle Ages sprang the chartered burghers of the earliest towns. From these burgesses the first elements of the bourgeoisie were developed.

The discovery of America, the rounding of the Cape, opened up fresh ground for the rising bourgeoisie. The East Indian and Chinese markets, the colonization of Amer-

ica, trade with the colonies, the increase in the means of
exchange and in commodities generally, gave to commerce,
to navigation, to industry, an impulse never before known,
and thereby, to the revolutionary element in the tottering
feudal society, a rapid development.

The feudal system of industry, under which industrial
production was monopolized by closed guilds, now no
longer sufficed for the growing wants of the new markets.
The manufacturing system took its place. The guildmasters
were pushed on one side by the manufacturing middle
class; division of labor between the different corporate
guilds vanished in the face of division of labor in each
single workshop.

Meantime the markets kept ever growing, the demand
ever rising. Even manufacture no longer sufficed. Thereupon, steam and machinery revolutionized industrial production. The place of manufacture was taken by the giant,
modern industry; the place of the industrial middle class by
industrial millionaires, the leaders of whole industrial armies, the modern bourgeois.

Modern industry has estabished the world market, for
which the discovery of America paved the way. This market has given an immense development to commerce, to
navigation, to communication by land. This development
has, in its turn, reacted on the extension of industry; and
in proportion as industry, commerce, navigation, railways
extended, in the same proportion the bourgeoisie developed, increased its capital, and pushed into the background
every class handed down from the Middle Ages.

We see, therefore, how the modern bourgeoisie is itself
the product of a long course of development, of a series of
revolutions in the modes of production and of exchange.

Each step in the development of the bourgeoisie was
accompanied by a corresponding political advance of that
class. An oppressed class under the sway of the feudal
nobility, an armed and self-governing association in the
medieval commune, here independent urban republic (as
in Italy and Germany), there taxable "third estate" of the
monarchy (as in France), afterwards, in the period of

manufacture proper, serving either the semi-feudal or the absolute monarchy as a counterpoise against the nobility and, in fact, cornerstone of the great monarchies in general, the bourgeoisie has at last, since the establishment of modern industry and of the world market, conquered for itself, in the modern representative State, exclusive political sway. The executive of the modern State is but a committee for managing the common affairs of the whole bourgeoisie.

The bourgeoisie, historically, has played a most revolutionary part.

The bourgeoisie, wherever it has got the upper hand, has put an end to all feudal, patriarchal, idyllic relations. It has pitilessly torn asunder the motley feudal ties that bound man to his "natural superiors," and has left remaining no other nexus between man and man than naked self-interest, than callous "cash payment." It has drowned the most heavenly ecstasies of religious fervor, of chivalrous enthusiasm, of philistine sentimentalism, in the icy water of egotistical calculation. It has resolved personal worth into exchange value, and in place of the numberless indefeasible chartered freedoms, has set up that single, unconscionable freedom—Free Trade. In one word, for exploitation, veiled by religious and political illusions, it has substituted naked, shameless, direct, brutal exploitation.

The bourgeoisie has stripped of its halo every occupation hitherto honored and looked up to with reverent awe. It has converted the physician, the lawyer, the priest, the poet, the man of science, into its paid wage-laborers.

The bourgeoisie has torn away from the family its sentimental veil, and has reduced the family relation to a mere money relation.

The bourgeoisie has disclosed how it came to pass that the brutal display of vigor in the Middle Ages, which reactionaries so much admire, found its fitting complement in the most slothful indolence. It has been the first to show what man's activity can bring about. It has accomplished wonders far surpassing Egyptian pyramids, Roman aqueducts, and Gothic cathedrals; it has conducted expeditions that put in the shade all former exoduses of nations and crusades.

The bourgeoisie cannot exist without constantly revolutionizing the instruments of production, and thereby the relations of production, and with them the whole relations of society. Conservation of the old modes of production in unaltered form, was, on the contrary, the first condition of existence for all earlier industrial classes. Constant revolutionizing of production, uninterrupted disturbance of all social conditions, everlasting uncertainty and agitation distinguish the bourgeois epoch from all earlier ones. All fixed, fast-frozen relations, with their train of ancient and venerable prejudices and opinions, are swept away, all newformed ones become antiquated before they can ossify. All that is solid melts into air, all that is holy is profaned, and man is at last compelled to face with sober senses his real conditions of life, and his relations with his kind.

The need of a constantly expanding market for its products chases the bourgeoisie over the whole surface of the globe. It must nestle everywhere, settle everywhere, establish connections everywhere.

The bourgeoisie has through its exploitation of the world market given a cosmopolitan character to production and consumption in every country. To the great chagrin of reactionaries, it has drawn from under the feet of industry the national ground on which it stood. All old-established national industries have been destroyed or are daily being destroyed. They are dislodged by new industries, whose introduction becomes a life and death question for all civilized nations, by industries that no longer work up indigenous raw material, but raw material drawn from the remotest zones; industries whose products are consumed, not only at home, but in every quarter of the globe. In place of the old wants, satisfied by the productions of the country, we find new wants, requiring for their satisfaction the products of distant lands and climes. In place of the old local and national seclusion and self-sufficiency, we have intercourse in every direction, universal interdependence of nations. And as in material, so also in intellectual production. The intellectual creations of individual nations become common property. National onesidedness and narrowmindedness become more and more impossible, and from the numerous national and local literatures, there arises a world literature.

The bourgeoisie, by the rapid improvement of all instruments of production, by the immensely facilitated means of communication, draws all, even the most barbarian, nations into civilization. The cheap prices of its commodities are the heavy artillery with which it batters down all Chinese walls, with which it forces the barbarians' intensely obstinate hatred of foreigners to capitulate. It compels all nations, on pain of extinction, to adopt the bourgeois mode of production; it compels them to introduce what it calls civilization into their midst, *i.e.*, to become bourgeois themselves. In one word, it creates a world after its own image.

The bourgeoisie has subjected the country to the rule of the towns. It has created enormous cities, has greately increased the urban population as compared with the rural, and has thus rescued a considerable part of the population from the idiocy of rural life. Just as it has made the country dependent on the towns, so it has made barbarian and semi-barbarian countries dependent on the civilized ones, nations of peasants on nations of bourgeois, the East on the West.

The bourgeoisie keeps more and more doing away with the scattered state of the population, of the means of production, and of property. It has agglomerated population, centralized means of production, and concentrated property in a few hands. The necessary consequence of this was political centralization. Independent, or but loosely connected, provinces with separate interests, laws, governments and systems of taxation, became lumped together into one nation, with one government, one code of laws, one national class interest, one frontier and one customs tariff.

The bourgeoisie, during its rule of scarce one hundred years, has created more massive and more colossal productive forces than have all preceding generations together. Subjection of Nature's forces to man, machinery, application of chemistry to industry and agriculture, steam navigation, railways, electric telegraphs, clearing of whole continents for cultivation, canalization of rivers, whole populations conjured out of the ground—what earlier century had even a presentiment that such productive forces slumbered in the lap of social labor?

We see then: the means of production and of exchange, on whose foundation the bourgeoisie built itself up, were generated in feudal society. At a certain stage in the development of these means of production and of exchange, the conditions under which feudal society produced and exchanged, the feudal organization of agriculture and manufacturing industry, in one word, the feudal relations of property became no longer compatible with the already developed productive forces; they became so many fetters. They had to be burst asunder; they were burst asunder.

Into their place stepped free competition, accompanied by a social and political constitution adapted to it, and by the economical and political sway of the bourgeois class.

A similar movement is going on before our own eyes. Modern bourgeois society with its relations of production, of exchange and of property, a society that has conjured up such gigantic means of production and of exchange, is like the sorcerer, who is no longer able to control the powers of the nether world whom he has called up by his spells. For many a decade past the history of industry and commerce is but the history of the revolt of modern productive forces against modern conditions of production, against the property relations that are the conditions for the existence of the bourgeoisie and of its rule. It is enough to mention the commercial crises that by their periodical return put on its trial, each time more threateningly, the existence of the entire bourgeois society. In these crises a great part not only of the existing products, but also of the previously created productive forces, are periodically destroyed. In these crises there breaks out an epidemic that, in all earlier epochs, would have seemed an absurdity—the epidemic of overproduction. Society suddenly finds itself put back into a state of momentary barbarism; it appears as if a famine, a universal war of devastation had cut off the supply of every means of subsistence; industry and commerce seem to be destroyed; and why? Because there is too much civilization, too much means of subsistence, too much industry, too much commerce. The productive forces at the disposal of society no longer tend to further the development of the conditions of bourgeois property; on the contrary, they have become too powerful for these conditions, by which they are fettered, and so soon as they overcome these fetters, they bring disorder into the whole of bourgeois society, endanger the existence of bourgeois property. The conditions of bourgeois society are too narrow to comprise the wealth created by them. And how does the bourgeoisie get over these crises? On the one hand by enforced destruction of a mass of productive forces; on the other, by the conquest of new markets, and by the more thorough exploitation of the old ones. That is to say, by paving the way for more extensive and more destructive crises, and by diminishing the means whereby crises are prevented.

The weapons with which the bourgeoisie felled feudalism to the ground are now turned against the bourgeoisie itself.

But not only has the bourgeoisie forged the weapons that bring death to itself; it has also called into existence the men who are to wield those weapons—the modern working class—the proletarians.

In proportion as the bourgeoisie, *i.e.*, capital, is developed, in the same proportion is the proletariat, the modern working class, developed—a class of laborers, who live only so long as they find work, and who find work only so long as their labor increases capital. These laborers, who must sell themselves piecemeal, are a commodity, like every other article of commerce, and are consequently exposed to all the vicissitudes of competition, to all the fluctuations of the market.

Owing to the extensive use of machinery and to division of labor, the work of the proletarians has lost all individual character, and, consequently, all charm for the workman. He becomes an appendage of the machine, and it is only the most simple, most monotonous, and most easily acquired knack, that is required of him. Hence, the cost of production of a workman is restricted, almost entirely, to the means of subsistence that he requires for his maintenance, and for the propagation of his race. But the price of a commodity, and therefore also of labor, is equal to its cost of production. In proportion, therefore, as the repulsiveness of the work increases, the wage decreases. Nay more, in proportion as the use of machinery and division of labor increases, in the same proportion the burden of toil also increases, whether by prolongation of the working hours, by increase of the work exacted in a given time or by increased speed of the machinery, etc.

Modern industry has converted the little workshop of the patriarchal master into the great factory of the industrial capitalist. Masses of laborers, crowded into the factory, are organized like soldiers. As privates of the industrial army they are placed under the command of a perfect hierarchy of officers and sergeants. Not only are they slaves of the bourgeois class, and of the bourgeois State; they are daily and hourly enslaved by the machine, by the overseer, and, above all, by the individual bourgeois manufacturer himself. The more openly this despotism proclaims gain to be its end and aim, the more petty, the more hateful and the more embittering it is.

The less the skill and exertion of strength implied in manual labor, in other words, the more modern industry becomes developed, the more is the labor of men superseded by that of women. Differences of age and sex have no longer any distinctive social validity for the working class. All are instruments of labor, more or less expensive to use, according to their age and sex.

No sooner is the exploitation of the laborer by the manufacturer so far at an end that he receives his wages in cash, than he is set upon by the other portions of the bourgeoisie, the landlord, the shopkeeper, the pawnbroker, etc.

The lower strata of the middle class—the small tradespeople, shopkeepers, and retired tradesmen generally, the handicraftsmen and peasants—all these sink gradually into the proletariat, partly because their diminutive capital does not suffice for the scale on which modern industry is carried on, and is swamped in the competition with the large capitalists, partly because their specialized skill is rendered worthless by new methods of production. Thus the proletariat is recruited from all classes of the population.

The proletariat goes through various stages of development. With its birth begins its struggle with the bourgeoisie. At first the contest is carried on by individual laborers, then by the workpeople of a factory, then by the operatives of one trade, in one locality, against the individual bourgeois who directly exploits them. They direct their attacks not against the bourgeois conditions of production, but against the instruments of production themselves; they destroy imported wares that compete with their labor, they smash to pieces machinery, they set factories ablaze, they seek to restore by force the vanished status of the workman of the Middle Ages.

At this stage the laborers still form an incoherent mass scattered over the whole country, and broken up by their mutual competition. If anywhere they unite to form more compact bodies, this is not yet the consequence of their own active union, but of the union of the bourgeoisie, which class, in order to attain its own political ends, is compelled to set the whole proletariat in motion, and is moreover yet, for a time, able to do so. At this stage, therefore, the proletarians do not fight their enemies, but the enemies of their enemies, the remnants of absolute monarchy, the landowners, the nonindustrial bourgeois, the petty bourgeoisie. Thus the whole historical movement is concentrated in the hands of the bourgeoisie; every victory so obtained is a victory for the bourgeoisie.

But with the development of industry the proletariat not only increases in number; it becomes concentrated in greater masses, its strength grows, and it feels that strength more. The various interests and conditions of life within the ranks of the proletariat are more and more equalized, in proportion as machinery obliterates all distinctions of labor, and nearly everywhere reduces wages to the same low level. The growing competition among the bourgeois, and the resulting commercial crises, make the wages of the workers ever more fluctuating. The unceasing improvement of machinery, ever more rapidly developing, makes their livelihood more and more precarious; the collisions between individual workmen and individual bourgeois take more and more the character of collisions between two classes. Thereupon the workers begin to form combinations (Trade Unions) against the bourgeois; they club together in order to keep up the rate of wages; they found permanent associations in order to make provision beforehand for these occasional revolts. Here and there the contest breaks out into riots.

Now and then the workers are victorious, but only for a time. The real fruit of their battles lies, not in the immediate result, but in the ever-expanding union of the workers. This union is helped on by the improved means of communication that are created by modern industry and that place the workers of different localities in contact with one another. It was just this contact that was needed to centralize the numerous local struggles, all of the same character, into one national struggle between classes. But every class struggle is a political struggle. And that union, to attain which the burghers of the Middle Ages, with their miserable highways, required centuries, the modern proletarians, thanks to railways, achieve in a few years.

This organization of the proletarians into a class, and consequently into a political party, is continually being upset again by the competition between the workers themselves. But it ever rises up again, stronger, firmer, mightier. It compels legislative recognition of particular interests of the workers, by taking advantage of the divisions among the bourgeoisie itself. Thus the ten-hours' bill in England was carried.

Altogether collisions between the classes of the old society further, in many ways, the course of development of the proletariat. The bourgeoisie finds itself involved in a constant battle. At first with the aristocracy; later on, with those portions of the bourgeoisie itself, whose interests have become antagonistic to the progress of industry; at all times, with the bourgeoisie of foreign countries. In all these battles it sees itself compelled to appeal to the proletariat, to ask for its help, and thus, to drag it into the political arena. The bourgeoisie itself, therefore, supplies the proletariat with its own elements of political and general education, in other words, it furnishes the proletariat with weapons for fighting the bourgeoisie.

Further, as we have already seen, entire sections of the ruling classes are, by the advance of industry, precipitated into the proletariat, or are at least threatened in their conditions of existence. These also supply the proletariat with fresh elements of enlightenment and progress.

Finally, in times when the class struggle nears the decisive hour, the process of dissolution going on within the ruling class, in fact within the whole range of old society, assumes such a violent, glaring character, that a small section of the ruling class cuts itself adrift, and joins the revolutionary class, the class that holds the future in its hands. Just as, therefore, at an earlier period, a section of the nobility went over to the bourgeoisie, so now a portion of the bourgeoisie goes over to the proletariat, and in particular, a portion of the bourgeois ideologists, who have raised themselves to the level of comprehending theoretically the historical movement as a whole.

Of all the classes that stand face to face with the bourgeoisie today, the proletariat alone is a really revolutionary class. The other classes decay and finally disappear in the face of modern industry; the proletariat is its special and essential product.

The lower middle class, the small manufacturer, the shopkeeper, the artisan, the peasant, all these fight against the bourgeoisie, to save from extinction their existence as fractions of the middle class. They are therefore not revolutionary, but conservative. Nay more, they are reactionary, for they try to roll back the wheel of history. If by chance they are revolutionary, they are so only in view of their impending transfer into the proletariat; they thus defend not their present, but their future interests, they desert their

own standpoint to place themselves at that of the proletariat.

The "dangerous class," the social scum, that passively
rotting mass thrown off by the lowest layers of old society,
may, here and there, be swept into the movement by a proletarian revolution; its conditions of life, however, prepare
it far more for the part of a bribed tool of reactionary
intrigue.

In the conditions of the proletariat, those of old society
at large are already virtually swamped. The proletarian is
without property; his relation to his wife and children has
no longer anything in common with the bourgeois family
relations; modern industrial labor, modern subjection to
capital, the same in England as in France, in America as in
Germany, has stripped him of every trace of national character. Law, morality, religion, are to him so many bourgeois prejudices, behind which lurk in ambush just as many
bourgeois interests.

All the preceding classes that got the upper hand, sought
to fortify their already acquired status by subjecting society at large to their conditions of appropriation. The proletarians cannot become masters of the productive forces
of society, except by abolishing their own previous mode
of appropriation, and thereby also every other previous
mode of appropriation. They have nothing of their own
to secure and to fortify; their mission is to destroy all previous securities for, and insurances of, individual property.

All previous historical movements were movements of
minorities, or in the interest of minorities. The proletarian
movement is the self-conscious, independent movement of
the immense majority, in the interest of the immense majority. The proletariat, the lowest stratum of our present
society, cannot stir, cannot raise itself up, without the
whole superincumbent strata of official society being sprung
into the air.

Though not in substance, yet in form, the struggle of
the proletariat with the bourgeoisie is at first a national
struggle. The proletariat of each country must, of course,
first of all settle matters with its own bourgeoisie.

In depicting the most general phases of the development of the proletariat, we traced the more or less veiled civil war, raging within existing society, up to the point where that war breaks out into open revolution, and where the violent overthrow of the bourgeoisie lays the foundation for the sway of the proletariat.

Hitherto, every form of society has been based, as we have already seen, on the antagonism of oppressing and oppressed classes. But in order to oppress a class, certain conditions must be assured to it under which it can, at least, continue its slavish existence. The serf, in the period of serfdom, raised himself to membership in the commune, just as the petty bourgeois, under the yoke of feudal absolutism, managed to develop into a bourgeois. The modern laborer, on the contrary, instead of rising with the progress of industry, sinks deeper and deeper below the conditions of existence of his own class. He becomes a pauper, and pauperism develops more rapidly than population and wealth. And here it becomes evident, that the bourgeoisie is unfit any longer to be the ruling class in society, and to impose its conditions of existence upon society as an overriding law. It is unfit to rule because it is incompetent to assure an existence to its slave within his slavery, because it cannot help letting him sink into such a state, that it has to feed him, instead of being fed by him. Society can no longer live under this bourgeoisie, in other words, its existence is no longer compatible with society.

The essential condition for the existence, and for the sway of the bourgeois class, is the formation and augmentation of capital; the condition for capital is wage labor. Wage labor rests exclusively on competition between the laborers. The advance of industry, whose involuntary promoter is the bourgeoisie, replaces the isolation of the laborers, due to competition, by their revolutionary combination, due to association. The development of modern industry, therefore, cuts from under its feet the very foundation on which the bourgeoisie produces and appropriates products. What the bourgeoisie, therefore, produces, above

all, is its own gravediggers. Its fall and the victory of the
proletariat are equally inevitable.

II. PROLETARIANS AND COMMUNISTS

In what relation do the Communists stand to the proletarians as a whole?

The Communists do not form a separate party opposed
to other working-class parties.

They have no interests separate and apart from those
of the proletariat as a whole.

They do not set up any sectarian principles of their own,
by which to shape and mold the proletarian movement.

The Communists are distinguished from the other working-class parties by this only: 1. In the national struggles
of the proletarians of the different countries, they point out
and bring to the front the common interests of the entire
proletariat, independently of all nationality. 2. In the various stages of development which the struggle of the working class against the bourgeoisie has to pass through, they
always and everywhere represent the interests of the movement as a whole.

The Communists, therefore, are on the one hand, practically, the most advanced and resolute section of the working-class parties of every country, that section which
pushes forward all others; on the other hand, theoretically,
they have over the great mass of the proletariat the advantage of clearly understanding the line of march, the
conditions, and the ultimate general results of the proletarian movement.

The immediate aim of the Communists is the same as
that of all the other proletarian parties: formation of the
proletariat into a class, overthrow of the bourgeois supremacy, conquest of political power by the proletariat.

The theoretical conclusions of the Communists are in no
way based on ideas or principles that have been invented,
or discovered, by this or that would-be universal reformer.

They merely express, in general terms, actual relations
springing from an existing class struggle, from a historical

movement going on under our very eyes. The abolition of existing property relations is not at all a distinctive feature of Communism.

All property relations in the past have continually been subject to historical change consequent upon the change in historical conditions.

The French Revolution, for example, abolished feudal property in favor of bourgeois property.

The distinguishing feature of Communism is not the abolition of property generally, but the abolition of bourgeois property. But modern bourgeois private property is the final and most complete expression of the system of producing and appropriating products, that is based on class antagonisms, on the exploitation of the many by the few.

In this sense, the theory of the Communists may be summed up in the single sentence: Abolition of private property.

We Communists have been reproached with the desire of abolishing the right of personally acquiring property as the fruit of a man's own labor, which property is alleged to be the groundwork of all personal freedom, activity and independence.

Hard-won, self-acquired, self-earned property! Do you mean the property of the petty artisan and of the small peasant, a form of property that preceded the bourgeois form? There is no need to abolish that; the development of industry has to a great extent already destroyed it, and is still destroying it daily.

Or do you mean modern bourgeois private property?

But does wage labor create any property for the laborer? Not a bit. It creates capital, *i.e.*, that kind of property which exploits wage labor, and which cannot increase except upon condition of begetting a new supply of wage labor for fresh exploitation. Property, in its present form, is based on the antagonism of capital and wage labor. Let us examine both sides of this antagonism.

To be a capitalist, is to have not only a purely personal, but a social *status* in production. Capital is a collective product, and only by the united action of many members, nay, in the last resort, only by the united action of all members of society, can it be set in motion.

Capital is, therefore, not a personal, it is a social power.

When, therefore, capital is converted into common property, into the property of all members of society, personal property is not thereby transformed into social property. It is only the social character of the property that is changed. It loses its class character.

Let us now take wage labor.

The average price of wage labor is the minimum wage, *i.e.,* that quantum of the means of subsistence, which is absolutely requisite to keep the laborer in bare existence as a laborer. What, therefore, the wage-laborer appropriates by means of his labor, merely suffices to prolong and reproduce a bare existence. We by no means intend to abolish this personal appropriation of the products of labor, an appropriation that is made for the maintenance and reproduction of human life, and that leaves no surplus wherewith to command the labor of others. All that we want to do away with is the miserable character of this appropriation, under which the laborer lives merely to increase capital, and is allowed to live only in so far as the interest of the ruling class requires it.

In bourgeois society, living labor is but a means to increase accumulated labor. In Communist society, accumulated labor is but a means to widen, to enrich, to promote the existence of the laborer.

In bourgeois society, therefore, the past dominates the present; in Communist society, the present dominates the past. In bourgeois society capital is independent and has individuality, while the living person is dependent and has no individuality.

And the abolition of this state of things is called by the bourgeois, abolition of individuality and freedom! And rightly so. The abolition of bourgeois individuality, bourgeois independence, and bourgeois freedom is undoubtedly aimed at.

By freedom is meant, under the present bourgeois conditions of production, free trade, free selling and buying.

But if selling and buying disappears, free selling and buying disappears also. This talk about free selling and buying, and all the other "brave words" of our bourgeoisie about freedom in general, have a meaning, if any, only in contrast with restricted selling and buying, with the fettered traders of the Middle Ages, but have no meaning when opposed to the Communistic abolition of buying and selling, of the bourgeois conditions of production, and of the bourgeoisie itself.

You are horrified at our intending to do away with private property. But in your existing society, private property is already done away with for nine-tenths of the population; its existence for the few is solely due to its nonexistence in the hands of those nine-tenths. You reproach us, therefore, with intending to do away with a form of property, the necessary condition for whose existence is, the nonexistence of any property for the immense majority of society.

In one word, you reproach us with intending to do away with your property. Precisely so; that is just what we intend.

From the moment when labor can no longer be converted into capital, money, or rent, into a social power capable of being monopolized, *i.e.*, from the moment when individual property can no longer be transformed into bourgeois property, into capital, from that moment, you say, individuality vanishes.

You must, therefore, confess that by "individual" you mean no other person than the bourgeois, than the middle-class owner of property. This person must, indeed, be swept out of the way, and made impossible.

Communism deprives no man of the power to appropriate the products of society; all that it does is to deprive him of the power to subjugate the labor of others by means of such appropriation.

It has been objected that upon the abolition of private

property all work will cease, and universal laziness will overtake us.

According to this, bourgeois society ought long ago to have gone to the dogs through sheer idleness; for those of its members who work, acquire nothing, and those who acquire anything, do not work. The whole of this objection is but another expression of the tautology: that there can no longer be any wage labor when there is no longer any capital.

All objections urged against the Communistic mode of producing and appropriating material products, have, in the same way, been urged against the Communistic modes of producing and appropriating intellectual products. Just as, to the bourgeois, the disappearance of class property is the disappearance of production itself, so the disappearance of class culture is to him identical with the disappearance of all culture.

That culture, the loss of which he laments, is, for the enormous majority, a mere training to act as a machine.

But don't wrangle with us so long as you apply, to our intended abolition of bourgeois property, the standard of your bourgeois notions of freedom, culture, law, etc. Your very ideas are but the outgrowth of the conditions of your bourgeois production and bourgeois property, just as your jurisprudence is but the will of your class made into a law for all, a will, whose essential character and direction are determined by the economical conditions of existence of your class.

The selfish misconception that induces you to transform into eternal laws of nature and of reason, the social forms springing from your present mode of production and form of property—historical relations that rise and disappear in the progress of production—this misconception you share with every ruling class that has preceded you. What you see clearly in the case of ancient property, what you admit in the case of feudal property, you are of course forbidden to admit in the case of your own bourgeois form of property.

Abolition of the family! Even the most radical flare up at this infamous proposal of the Communists.

On what foundation is the present family, the bourgeois family, based? On capital, on private gain. In its completely developed form this family exists only among the bourgeoisie. But this state of things finds its complement in the practical absence of the family among the proletarians, and in public prostitution.

The bourgeois family will vanish as a matter of course when its complement vanishes, and both will vanish with the vanishing of capital.

Do you charge us with wanting to stop the exploitation of children by their parents? To this crime we plead guilty.

But, you will say, we destroy the most hallowed of relations, when we replace home education by social.

And your education! Is not that also social, and determined by the social conditions under which you educate, by the intervention, direct or indirect, of society, by means of schools, etc.? The Communists have not invented the intervention of society in education; they do but seek to alter the character of that intervention, and to rescue education from the influence of the ruling class.

The bourgeois claptrap about the family and education, about the hallowed co-relation of parent and child, becomes all the more disgusting, the more, by the action of modern industry, all family ties among the proletarians are torn asunder, and their children transformed into simple articles of commerce and instruments of labor.

But you Communists would introduce community of women, screams the whole bourgeoisie in chorus.

The bourgeois sees in his wife a mere instrument of production. He hears that the instruments of production are to be exploited in common, and, naturally, can come to no other conclusion than that the lot of being common to all will likewise fall to the women.

He has not even a suspicion that the real point aimed at is to do away with the status of women as mere instruments of production.

For the rest, nothing is more ridiculous than the virtuous indignation of our bourgeois at the community of women which, they pretend, is to be openly and officially established by the Communists. The Communists have no need to introduce community of women; it has existed almost from time immemorial.

Our bourgeois, not content with having the wives and daughters of their proletarians at their disposal, not to speak of common prostitutes, take the greatest pleasure in seducing each other's wives.

Bourgeois marriage is in reality a system of wives in common and thus, at the most, what the Communists might possibly be reproached with, is that they desire to introduce, in substitution for a hypocritically concealed, an openly legalized community of women. For the rest, it is self-evident that the abolition of the present system of production must bring with it the abolition of the community of women springing from that system, *i.e.*, of prostitution both public and private.

The Communists are further reproached with desiring to abolish countries and nationality.

The working men have no country. We cannot take from them what they have not got. Since the proletariat must first of all acquire political supremacy, must rise to be the leading class of the nation, must constitute itself *the* nation, it is, so far, itself national, though not in the bourgeois sense of the word.

National differences and antagonisms between peoples are daily more and more vanishing, owing to the development of the bourgeoisie, to freedom of commerce, to the world market, to uniformity in the mode of production and in the conditions of life corresponding thereto.

The supremacy of the proletariat will cause them to vanish still faster. United action, of the leading civilized countries at least, is one of the first conditions for the emancipation of the proletariat.

In proportion as the exploitation of one individual by another is put an end to, the exploitation of one nation by another will also be put an end to. In proportion as the antagonism between classes within the nation vanishes, the hostility of one nation to another will come to an end.

The charges against Communism made from a religious, a philosophical, and, generally, from an ideological standpoint, are not deserving of serious examination.

Does it require deep intuition to comprehend that man's ideas, views and conceptions, in one word, man's consciousness, changes with every change in the conditions of his material existence, in his social relations and in his social life?

What else does the history of ideas prove, than that intellectual production changes its character in proportion as material production is changed? The ruling ideas of each age have ever been the ideas of its ruling class.

When people speak of ideas that revolutionize society, they do but express the fact, that within the old society, the elements of a new one have been created, and that the dissolution of the old ideas keeps even pace with the dissolution of the old conditions of existence.

When the ancient world was in its last throes, the ancient religions were overcome by Christianity. When Christian ideas succumbed in the 18th century to rationalist ideas, feudal society fought its death battle with the then revolutionary bourgeoisie. The ideas of religious liberty and freedom of conscience merely gave expression to the sway of free competition within the domain of knowledge.

"Undoubtedly," it will be said, "religious, moral, philosophical and juridical ideas have been modified in the course of historical development. But religion, morality, philosophy, political science, and law, constantly survived this change.

"There are, besides, eternal truths, such as Freedom, Justice, etc., that are common to all states of society. But Communism abolishes eternal truths, it abolishes all religion, and all morality, instead of constituting them on a new basis; it therefore acts in contradiction to all past historical experience."

What does this accusation reduce itself to? The history of all past society has consisted in the development of class antagonisms, antagonisms that assumed different forms at different epochs.

But whatever form they may have taken, one fact is common to all past ages, *viz.*, the exploitation of one part of society by the other. No wonder, then, that the social consciousness of past ages, despite all the multiplicity and variety it displays, moves within certain common forms, or general ideas, which cannot completely vanish except with the total disappearance of class antagonisms.

The Communist revolution is the most radical rupture with traditional property relations; no wonder that its development involves the most radical rupture with traditional ideas.

But let us have done with the bourgeois objections to Communism.

We have seen above, that the first step in the revolution by the working class, is to raise the proletariat to the position of ruling class, to win the battle of democracy.

The proletariat will use its political supremacy to wrest, by degrees, all capital from the bourgeoisie, to centralize all instruments of production in the hands of the State, *i.e.*, of the proletariat organized as the ruling class; and to increase the total of productive forces as rapidly as possible.

Of course, in the beginning, this cannot be effected except by means of despotic inroads on the rights of property, and on the conditions of bourgeois production; by means of measures, therefore, which appear economically insufficient and untenable, but which, in the course of the movement, outstrip themselves, necessitate further inroads upon the old social order, and are unavoidable as a means of entirely revolutionizing the mode of production.

These measures will of course be different in different countries.

Nevertheless in the most advanced countries, the following will be pretty generally applicable.

1. Abolition of property in land and application of all rents of land to public purposes.

2. A heavy progressive or graduated income tax.

3. Abolition of all right of inheritance.

4. Confiscation of the property of all emigrants and rebels.

5. Centralization of credit in the hands of the State, by means of a national bank with State capital and an exclusive monopoly.

6. Centralization of the means of communication and transport in the hands of the State.

7. Extension of factories and instruments of production owned by the State; the bringing into cultivation of waste-lands, and the improvement of the soil generally in accordance with a common plan.

8. Equal liability of all to labor. Establishment of industrial armies, especially for agriculture.

9. Combination of agriculture with manufacturing industries; gradual abolition of the distinction between town and country, by a more equable distribution of the population over the country.

10. Free education for all children in public schools. Abolition of children's factory labor in its present form. Combination of education with industrial production, etc., etc.

When, in the course of development, class distinctions have disappeared, and all production has been concentrated in the hands of a vast association of the whole nation, the public power will lose its political character. Political power, properly so called, is merely the organized power of one class for oppressing another. If the proletariat during its contest with the bourgeoisie is compelled, by the force of circumstances, to organize itself as a class, if, by means of a revolution, it makes itself the ruling class, and, as such, sweeps away by force the old conditions of production, then it will, along with these conditions, have swept away the conditions for the existence of class antagonisms and of classes generally, and will thereby have abolished its own supremacy as a class.

In place of the old bourgeois society, with its classes and class antagonisms, we shall have an association, in which the free development of each is the condition for the free development of all. . . .

IV. POSITION OF THE COMMUNISTS . . .

. . . the Communists everywhere support every revolutionary movement against the existing social and political order of things.

In all these movements they bring to the front, as the leading question in each, the property question, no matter what its degree of development at the time.

Finally, they labor everywhere for the union and agreement of the democratic parties of all countries.

The Communists disdain to conceal their views and aims. They openly declare that their ends can be attained only by the forcible overthrow of all existing social conditions. Let the ruling classes tremble at a Communistic revolution. The proletarians have nothing to lose but their chains. They have a world to win.

WORKINGMEN OF ALL COUNTRIES, UNITE!

MARX: THE MATERIALIST INTERPRETATION OF HISTORY

Marx succinctly outlined his theory of historical evolution in his introduction to A Contribution to the Critique of Political Economy, *published in 1859—the first major work he completed after moving to England. Engels later coined the term "historical materialism" to describe this theory.*

A CONTRIBUTION TO THE CRITIQUE OF POLITICAL ECONOMY

I was led by my studies to the conclusion that legal relations as well as forms of state could be neither understood by themselves nor explained by the so-called general progress of the human mind, but that they are rooted in the material conditions of life, which are summed up by Hegel after the fashion of the English and French of the eighteenth century under the name "civil society"; the anatomy of that civil society is to be sought in political economy. The study of the latter, which I had taken up in Paris, I continued at Brussels, whither I immigrated on account of an order of expulsion issued by Mr. Guizot. The general conclusion at which I arrived and which, once reached, continued to serve as the leading thread in my studies may be briefly summed up as follows: In the social production which men carry on they enter into definite relations that are indispensable and independent of their will; these relations of production correspond to a definite stage of development of their material powers of production. The sum total of these relations of production constitutes the economic structure of society—the real foundation, on which rise legal and political superstructures and to which correspond definite forms of social consciousness. The mode of production in material life determines the general characters of the social, political, and spiritual processes of life. It is not the consciousness of men that

From Karl Marx, *A Contribution to the Critique of Political Economy,* translated by N. I. Stone (New York, International Library Publishing Co., 1904), pp. 11-13.

determines their existence, but, on the contrary, their
social existence determines their consciousness. At a certain
stage of their development the material forces of production in society come into conflict with the existing relations
of production, or—what is but a legal expression for the
same thing—with the property relations within which they
had been at work before. From forms of development of
the forces of production these relations turn into their
fetters. Then comes the period of social revolution. With
the change of the economic foundation the entire immense
superstructure is more or less rapidly transformed. In considering such transformations the distinction should always
be made between the material transformation of the economic conditions of production, which can be determined
with the precision of natural science, and the legal, political, religious, aesthetic, or philosophic—in short, ideological—forms in which men become conscious of this
conflict and fight it out. Just as our opinion of an individual
is not based on what he thinks of himself, so can we not
judge such a period of transformation by its own consciousness; on the contrary, this consciousness must rather be
explained from the contradictions of material life, from the
existing conflict between the social forces of production
and the relations of production. No social order ever disappears before all the productive forces for which there is
room in it have been developed, and new, higher relations
of production never appear before the material conditions
of their existence have matured in the womb of the old
society. Therefore mankind always takes up only such
problems as it can solve, since, looking at the matter more
closely, we will always find that the problem itself arises
only when the material conditions necessary for its solution
already exist or are at least in the process of formation. In
broad outlines we can designate the Asiatic, the ancient,
the feudal, and the modern bourgeois methods of production as so many epochs in the progress of the economic
formation of society. The bourgeois relations of production
are the last antagonistic form of the social process of production—antagonistic not in the sense of individual an-

tagonism, but of one arising from conditions surrounding the life of individuals in society; at the same time the productive forces developing in the womb of bourgeois society create the material conditions for the solution of that antagonism. This social formation constitutes, therefore, the closing chapter of the prehistoric stage of human society. . . .

MARX: THE THEORY OF CAPITALISM

Marx's most famous work is Das Kapital—*"Capital"—a mammoth treatise on the development, operation, and anticipated breakdown of the capitalist economic system. Volume I was published in 1867, but Marx did not complete the work, and the remaining two volumes had to be edited and published after his death.*

The following selection is taken largely from two chapters near the end of Volume I (Chapter XXV, "The General Law of Capitalist Accumulation," and Chapter XXXII, "The Historical Tendency of Capitalistic Accumulation"), in which Marx brings together his main arguments concerning "surplus value," the exploitation and misery of the proletariat, and the inevitability of revolution. Marx did not close his eyes to the possibility of reform within capitalism, however, as the opening passage below from his preface indicates.

CAPITAL

PREFACE

. . . In this work I have to examine the capitalist mode of production, and the conditions of production and exchange corresponding to that mode. Up to the present time, their classic ground is England. That is the reason why England is used as the chief illustration in the development of my theoretical ideas. If, however, the German reader shrugs his shoulders at the condition of the English industrial and agricultural laborers, or in optimist fashion comforts himself with the thought that in Germany things are not nearly so bad, I must plainly tell him, *"De te fabula narratur!"*

Intrinsically, it is not a question of the higher or lower degree of development of the social antagonisms that result from the natural laws of capitalist production. It is a question of these laws themselves, of these tendencies working with iron necessity towards inevitable results. The country that is more developed industrially only shows, to the less developed, the image of its own future.

From Karl Marx, *Capital* (New York, Modern Library, n.d.), pp. 13-15, 671-673, 678-681, 707-709, 834-837.

But apart from this. Where capitalist production is fully naturalized among the Germans (for instance, in the factories proper) the condition of things is much worse than in England, because the counterpoise of the Factory Acts is wanting. In all other spheres, we, like all the rest of Continental Western Europe, suffer not only from the developing of capitalist production, but also from the incompleteness of that development. Alongside of modern evils, a whole series of inherited evils oppress us, arising from the passive survival of antiquated modes of production, with their inevitable train of social and political anachronisms. We suffer not only from the living, but from the dead. *Le mort saisit le vif!*

The social statistics of Germany and the rest of Continental Western Europe are, in comparison with those of England, wretchedly compiled. But they raise the veil just enough to let us catch a glimpse of the Medusa head behind it. We should be appalled at the state of things at home, if, as in England, our governments and parliaments appointed periodically commissions of enquiry into economic conditions; if these commissions were armed with the same plenary powers to get at the truth; if it was possible to find for this purpose men as competent, as free from partisanship and respect of persons as are the English factory-inspectors, her medical reporters on public health, her commissioners of enquiry into the exploitation of women and children, into housing and food. Perseus wore a magic cap that the monsters he hunted down might not see him. We draw the magic cap down over eyes and ears as a make-believe that there are no monsters. Let us not deceive ourselves on this. As in the 18th century, the American war of independence sounded the tocsin for the European middle class, so in the 19th century, the American civil war sounded it for the European working class. In England the progress of social disintegration is palpable. When it has reached a certain point, it must react on the continent. There it will take a form more brutal or more humane, according to the degree of development of the working class itself. Apart from higher motives, therefore, their own most important interests dictate to the classes that are for the nonce the ruling ones, the removal of all legally removable hindrances to the free development of the working class. For this reason, as well as others, I have given so large a space in this volume to the history, the details, and the results of English factory legislation. One nation can and should learn from others. And even when a society has got upon the right track for the discovery of the natural laws of its movement—and it is the ultimate aim of this work, to lay bare the economic law of motion of modern society—it can neither clear by bold leaps, nor remove by legal enactments, the obstacles offered by the successive phases of its normal development. But it can shorten and lessen the birth pangs.

To prevent possible misunderstanding, a word. I paint the capitalist and the landlord in no sense *couleur de rose*. But here individuals are dealt with only in so far as they are the personifications of economic categories, embodiments of particular class-relations and class-interests. My standpoint, from which the evolution of the economic formation of society is viewed as a process of natural history, can less than any other make the individual responsible for relations whose creature he socially remains, however much he may subjectively raise himself above them. . . .

XXV. THE GENERAL LAW OF CAPITALIST ACCUMULATION.

*The Increased Demand for Labor-Power that
Accompanies Accumulation, the Composition of
Capital Remaining the Same.*

In this chapter we consider the influence of the growth of capital on the lot of the laboring class. The most important factor in this inquiry is the composition of capital and the change it undergoes in the course of the process of accumulation.

The composition of capital is to be understood in a two-fold sense. On the side of value, it is determined by the proportion in which it is divided into constant capital or value of the means of production, and variable capital or value of labor-power, the sum total of wages. On the side of material, as it functions in the process of production, all capital is divided into means of production and living labor-power. This latter composition is determined by the relation between the mass of the means of production employed, on the one hand, and the mass of labor necessary for their employment on the other. I call the former the *value composition*, the latter the *technical composition* of capital. Between the two there is a strict correlation. To express this, I call the value composition of capital, in so far as it is determined by its technical composition and mirrors the changes of the latter, the *organic composition* of capital. Wherever I refer to the composition of capital, without further qualification, its organic composition is always understood.

The many individual capitals invested in a particular branch of production have, one with another, more or less different compositions. The average of their individual compositions gives us the composition of the total capital in this branch of production. Lastly, the average of these averages, in all branches of production, gives us the composition of the total social capital of a country, and with this alone are we, in the last resort, concerned in the following investigation.

Growth of capital involves growth of its variable constituent or of the part invested in labor-power. A part of the surplus value turned into additional capital must always be retransformed into variable capital, or additional labor-fund. If we suppose that, all other circumstances remaining the same, the composition of capital also remains constant (*i.e.*, that a definite mass of means of production constantly needs the same mass of labor-power to set in motion,) then the demand for labor and the subsistence-fund of the laborers clearly increase in the same proportion as the capital, and the more rapidly, the more rapidly the capital increases. Since the capital produces yearly a surplus value, of which one part is yearly added to the original capital; since this increment itself grows yearly along

with the augmentation of the capital already functioning; since lastly, under special stimulus to enrichment, such
as the opening of new markets, or of new spheres for the
outlay of capital in consequence of newly developed social
wants, etc., the scale of accumulation may be suddenly
extended, merely by a change in the division of the surplus value or surplus product into capital and revenue, the
requirements of accumulating capital may exceed the increase of labor-power or of the number of laborers; the
demand for laborers may exceed the supply, and, therefore, wages may rise. This must, indeed, ultimately be the
case if the conditions supposed above continue. For since
in each year more laborers are employed than in its prede-
cessor, sooner or later a point must be reached, at which
the requirements of accumulation begin to surpass the
customary supply of labor, and, therefore, a rise of wages
takes place. A lamentation on this score was heard in England during the whole of the fifteenth, and the first half
of the eighteenth centuries. The more or less favorable
circumstances in which the wage-working class supports
and multiplies itself in no way alter the fundamental character of capitalist production. As simple reproduction constantly reproduces the capital relation itself, *i.e.*, the
relation of capitalists on the one hand, and wage-workers
on the other, so reproduction on a progressive scale, *i.e.*,
accumulation, reproduces the capital relation on a progressive scale, more capitalists or larger capitalists at this pole,
more wage-workers at that. The reproduction of a mass of
labor-power, which must incessantly reincorporate itself
with capital for that capital's self-expansion; which cannot
get free from capital, and whose enslavement to capital
is only concealed by the variety of individual capitalists
to whom it sells itself, this reproduction of labor-power
forms, in fact, an essential of the reproduction of capital
itself. Accumulation of capital is, therefore, increase of the
proletariat. . . .

. . . Labor-power is sold today, not with a view of satisfying, by its service or by its product, the personal needs
of the buyer. His aim is augmentation of his capital, pro-

duction of commodities containing more labor than he pays for, containing therefore a portion of value that costs him nothing, and that is nevertheless realized when the commodities are sold. Production of surplus value is the absolute law of this mode of production. Labor-power is only saleable so far as it preserves the means of production in their capacity of capital, reproduces its own value as capital, and yields in unpaid labor a source of additional capital. The conditions of its sale, whether more or less favorable to the laborer, include therefore the necessity of its constant reselling, and the constantly extended reproduction of all wealth in the shape of capital. Wages, as we have seen, by their very nature, always imply the performance of a certain quantity of unpaid labor on the part of the laborer. Altogether, irrespective of the case of a rise of wages with a falling price of labor, etc., such an increase only means at best a quantitative diminution of the unpaid labor that the worker has to supply. This diminution can never reach the point at which it would threaten the system itself. Apart from violent conflicts as to the rate of wages (and Adam Smith has already shown that in such a conflict, taken on the whole, the master is always master), a rise in the price of labor resulting from accumulation of capital implies the following alternative:

Either the price of labor keeps on rising, because its rise does not interfere with the progress of accumulation. In this there is nothing wonderful, for, says Adam Smith, "after these (profits) are diminished, stock may not only continue to increase, but to increase much faster than before. . . . A great stock, though with small profits, generally increases faster than a small stock with great profits." In this case it is evident that a diminution in the unpaid labor in no way interferes with the extension of the domain of capital.—Or, on the other hand, accumulation slackens in consequence of the rise in the price of labor, because the stimulus of gain is blunted. The rate of accumulation lessens; but with its lessening, the primary cause of that lessening vanishes, *i.e.*, the disproportion between capital and exploitable labor-power. The mechanism of the process

of capitalist production removes the very obstacles that it
temporarily creates. The price of labor falls again to a level
corresponding with the needs of the self-expansion of
capital, whether the level be below, the same as, or above
the one which was normal before the rise of wages took
place. We see thus: In the first case, it is not the diminished rate either of the absolute, or of the proportional,
increase in labor-power, or laboring population, which
causes capital to be in excess, but conversely the excess
of capital that makes exploitable labor-power insufficient.
In the second case, it is not the increased rate either of the
absolute, or of the proportional, increase in labor-power,
or laboring population, that makes capital insufficient; but,
conversely, the relative diminution of capital that causes
the exploitable labor-power, or rather its price, to be in
excess. It is these absolute movements of the accumulation
of capital which are reflected as relative movements of the
mass of exploitable labor-power, and therefore seem produced by the latter's own independent movement. To put
it mathematically: the rate of accumulation is the independent, not the dependent, variable; the rate of wages,
the dependent, not the independent, variable. Thus, when
the industrial cycle is in the phase of crisis, a general fall
in the price of commodities is expressed as a rise in the
value of money, and, in the phase of prosperity, a general
rise in the price of commodities, as a fall in the value of
money. The so-called currency school concludes from this
that with high prices too little, with low prices too much
money is in circulation. Their ignorance and complete misunderstanding of facts are worthily paralleled by the
economists, who interpret the above phenomena of accumulation by saying that there are now too few, now too
many wage laborers.

The law of capitalist production, that is at the bottom
of the pretended "natural law of population," reduces itself simply to this: The correlation between accumulation
of capital and rate of wages is nothing else than the correlation between the unpaid labor transformed into capital,
and the additional paid labor necessary for the setting in

motion of this additional capital. It is therefore in no way a relation between two magnitudes, independent one of the other: on the one hand, the magnitude of the capital; on the other, the number of the laboring population; it is rather, at bottom, only the relation between the unpaid and the paid labor of the same laboring population. If the quantity of unpaid labor supplied by the working class, and accumulated by the capitalist class, increases so rapidly that its conversion into capital requires an extraordinary addition of paid labor, then wages rise, and, all other circumstances remaining equal, the unpaid labor diminishes in proportion. But as soon as this diminution touches the point at which the surplus labor that nourishes capital is no longer supplied in normal quantity, a reaction sets in: a smaller part of revenue is capitalized, accumulation lags, and the movement of rise in wages receives a check. The rise of wages therefore is confined within limits that not only leave intact the foundations of the capitalistic system, but also secure its reproduction on a progressive scale. The law of capitalistic accumulation, metamorphosed by economists into a pretended law of nature, in reality merely states that the very nature of accumulation excludes every diminution in the degree of exploitation of labor, and every rise in the price of labor, which could seriously imperil the continual reproduction, on an ever enlarging scale, of the capitalistic relation. It cannot be otherwise in a mode of production in which the laborer exists to satisfy the needs of self-expansion of existing values, instead of on the contrary, material wealth existing to satisfy the needs of development on the part of the laborer. As, in religion, man is governed by the products of his own brain, so in capitalistic production, he is governed by the products of his own hand. . . .

Different Forms of the Relative Surplus Population.
The General Law of Capitalistic Accumulation.

. . . The greater the social wealth, the functioning capital, the extent and energy of its growth, and, therefore, also

the absolute mass of the proletariat and the productiveness of its labor, the greater is the industrial reserve army.
The same causes which develop the expansive power of
capital, develop also the labor-power at its disposal. The
relative mass of the industrial reserve army increases therefore with the potential energy of wealth. But the greater
this reserve army in proportion to the active labor army,
the greater is the mass of a consolidated surplus population, whose misery is in inverse ratio to its torment of labor.
The more extensive, finally, the lazarus-layers of the working class, and the industrial reserve army, the greater is
official pauperism. *This is the absolute general law of
capitalist accumulation.* Like all other laws it is modified
in its working by many circumstances, the analysis of
which does not concern us here.

The folly is now patent of the economic wisdom that
preaches to the laborers the accommodation of their number to the requirements of capital. The mechanism of
capitalist production and accumulation constantly effects
this adjustment. The first word of this adaptation is the
creation of a relative surplus population, or industrial
reserve army. Its last word is the misery of constantly
extending strata of the active army of labor, and the dead
weight of pauperism.

The law by which a constantly increasing quantity of
means of production, thanks to the advance in the productiveness of social labor, may be set in movement by a
progressively diminishing expenditure of human power,
this law, in a capitalist society—where the laborer does not
employ the means of production, but the means of production employ the laborer—undergoes a complete inversion
and is expressed thus: the higher the productiveness of
labor, the greater is the pressure of the laborers on the
means of employment, the more precarious, therefore,
becomes their condition of existence, viz., the sale of their
own labor-power for the increasing of another's wealth, or
for the self-expansion of capital. The fact that the means
of production, and the productiveness of labor, increase

more rapidly than the productive population, expresses itself, therefore, capitalistically in the inverse form that the laboring population always increases more rapidly than the conditions under which capital can employ this increase for its own self-expansion.

We saw in Part IV., when analyzing the production of relative surplus value: within the capitalist system all methods for raising the social productiveness of labor are brought about at the cost of the individual laborer; all means for the development of production transform themselves into means of domination over, and exploitation of, the producers; they mutilate the laborer into a fragment of a man, degrade him to the level of an appendage of a machine, destroy every remnant of charm in his work and turn it into a hated toil; they estrange from him the intellectual potentialities of the labor-process in the same proportion as science is incorporated in it as an independent power; they distort the conditions under which he works, subject him during the labor process to a despotism the more hateful for its meanness; they transform his lifetime into working time, and drag his wife and child beneath the wheels of the Juggernaut of capital. But all methods for the production of surplus value are at the same time methods of accumulation; and every extension of accumulation becomes again a means for the development of those methods. It follows therefore that in proportion as capital accumulates, the lot of the laborer, be his payment high or low, must grow worse. The law, finally, that always equilibrates the relative surplus population, or industrial reserve army, to the extent and energy of accumulation, this law rivets the laborer to capital more firmly than the wedges of Vulcan did Prometheus to the rock. It establishes an accumulation of misery, corresponding with accumulation of capital. Accumulation of wealth at one pole is, therefore, at the same time accumulation of misery, agony of toil, slavery, ignorance, brutality, mental degradation, at the opposite pole, *i.e.*, on the side of the class that produces its own product in the form of capital. . . .

XXXII. HISTORICAL TENDENCY OF
CAPITALIST ACCUMULATION

What does the primitive accumulation of capital, *i.e.*, its historical genesis, resolve itself into? In so far as it is not immediate transformation of slaves and serfs into wage-laborers, and therefore a mere change of form, it only means the expropriation of the immediate producers, *i.e.*, the dissolution of private property based on the labor of its owner. Private property, as the antithesis to social, collective property, exists only where the means of labor and the external conditions of labor belong to private individuals. But according as these private individuals are laborers or not laborers, private property has a different character. The numberless shades, that it at first sight presents, correspond to the intermediate stages lying between these two extremes. The private property of the laborer in his means of production is the foundation of petty industry, whether agricultural, manufacturing or both; petty industry, again, is an essential condition for the development of social production and of the free individuality of the laborer himself. Of course, this petty mode of production exists also under slavery, serfdom, and other states of dependence. But it flourishes, it lets loose its whole energy, it attains its adequate classical form, only where the laborer is the private owner of his own means of labor set in action by himself: the peasant of the land which he cultivates, the artisan of the tool which he handles as a virtuoso. This mode of production presupposes parceling of the soil, and scattering of the other means of production. As it excludes the concentration of these means of production, so also it excludes cooperation, division of labor within each separate process of production, the control over, and the productive application of the forces of Nature by society, and the free development of the social productive powers. It is compatible only with a system of production, and a society, moving within narrow and more or less primitive bounds. To perpetuate it would be, as Pecqueur rightly says, "to decree universal mediocrity."

At a certain stage of development it brings forth the material agencies for its own dissolution. From that moment new forces and new passions spring up in the bosom of society; but the old social organization fetters them and keeps them down. It must be annihilated; it is annihilated. Its annihilation, the transformation of the individualized and scattered means of production into socially concentrated ones, of the pigmy property of the many into the huge property of the few, the expropriation of the great mass of the people from the soil, from the means of subsistence, and from the means of labor, this fearful and painful expropriation of the mass of the people forms the prelude to the history of capital. It comprises a series of forcible methods, of which we have passed in review only those that have been epochmaking as methods of the primitive accumulation of capital. The expropriation of the immediate producers was accomplished with merciless vandalism, and under the stimulus of passions the most infamous, the most sordid, the pettiest, the most meanly odious. Self-earned private property, that is based, so to say, on the fusing together of the isolated, independent laboring individual with the conditions of his labor, is supplanted by capitalistic private property, which rests on exploitation of the nominally free labor of others, *i.e.*, on wage-labor.

As soon as this process of transformation has sufficiently decomposed the old society from top to bottom, as soon as the laborers are turned into proletarians, their means of labor into capital, as soon as the capitalist mode of production stands on its own feet, then the further socialization of labor and further transformation of the land and other means of production into socially exploited and, therefore, common means of production, as well as the further expropriation of private proprietors, takes a new form. That which is now to be expropriated is no longer the laborer working for himself, but the capitalist exploiting many laborers. This expropriation is accomplished by the action of the immanent laws of capitalistic production itself, by the centralization of capital. One capitalist always kills

many. Hand in hand with this centralization, or this expropriation of many capitalists by few, develop, on an
ever extending scale, the cooperative form of the labor-
process, the conscious technical application of science, the
methodical cultivation of the soil, the transformation of the
instruments of labor into instruments of labor only usable
in common, the economizing of all means of production by
their use as the means of production of combined, socialized labor, the entanglement of all peoples in the net of
the world market, and this, the international character of
the capitalistic régime. Along with the constantly diminishing number of the magnates of capital, who usurp and
monopolize all advantages of this process of transformation,
grows the mass of misery, oppression, slavery, degradation,
exploitation; but with this too grows the revolt of the
working class, a class always increasing in numbers, and
disciplined, united, organized by the very mechanism of the
process of capitalist production itself. The monopoly of
capital becomes a fetter upon the mode of production,
which has sprung up and flourished along with, and under
it. Centralization of the means of production and socialization of labor at last reach a point where they become
incompatible with their capitalist integument. This integument is burst asunder. The knell of capitalist private property sounds. The expropriators are expropriated.

The capitalist mode of appropriation, the result of the
capitalist mode of production, produces capitalist private
property. This is the first negation of individual private
property, as founded on the labor of the proprietor. But
capitalist production begets, with the inexorability of a law
of nature, its own negation. It is the negation of negation.
This does not re-establish private property for the producer, but gives him individual property based on the ac-
quisitions of the capitalist era: *i.e.*, on cooperation and the
possession in common of the land and of the means of
production.

The transformation of scattered private property, arising
from individual labor, into capitalist private property is,
naturally, a process incomparably more protracted, violent,

and difficult, than the transformation of capitalistic private property, already practically resting on socialized production, into socialized property. In the former case, we had the expropriation of the mass of the people by a few usurpers; in the latter, we have the expropriation of a few usurpers by the mass of the people.

ENGELS: THE DIALECTICAL PHILOSOPHY

*After the mid-1870's Marx was too ill to write much more, and
Engels began to publish extensively on his own. Where Marx's
emphasis had been economic, Engels was more inclined to phi-
losophy. In 1876 he published a long polemical book to refute
the theories of another German socialist, under the title,* Herr
Eugen Dühring's Revolution in Science. *Better known as the*
Anti-Dühring, *this work set forth the philosophical combination
of Hegel's dialectic with the doctrine of scientific materialism.
Plekhanov later termed this amalgam "dialectical materialism."
It is still the official philosophical position of Communism.*

ANTI-DÜHRING

. . . When we consider and reflect upon nature at large or
the history of mankind or our own intellectual activity, at
first we see the picture of an endless entanglement of relations and reactions, permutations and combinations, in
which nothing remains what, where and as it was, but
everything moves, changes, comes into being and passes
away. This primitive, naive but intrinsically correct conception of the world is that of ancient Greek philosophy,
and was first clearly formulated by Heraclitus: everything
is and is not, for everything is *fluid,* is constantly changing,
constantly coming into being and passing away.

But this conception, correctly as it expresses the general
character of the picture of appearances as a whole, does
not suffice to explain the details of which this picture is
made up, and so long as we do not understand these, we
have not a clear idea of the whole picture. In order to
understand these details we must detach them from their
natural or historical connection and examine each one
separately, its nature, special causes, effects, etc. This is,
primarily, the task of natural science and historical research: branches of science which the Greeks of classical
times, on very good grounds, relegated to a subordinate
position, because they had first of all to collect materials.

From Friedrich Engels, *Anti-Dühring* (Moscow, Foreign Languages Publishing House, 1954), pp. 33-43.

The foundations of the exact natural sciences were first worked out by the Greeks of the Alexandrian period, and later on, in the Middle Ages, by the Arabs. Real natural science dates from the second half of the fifteenth century, and thence onward it had advanced with constantly increasing rapidity. The analysis of nature into its individual parts, the grouping of the different natural processes and objects in definite classes, the study of the internal anatomy of organic bodies in their manifold forms —these were the fundamental conditions of the gigantic strides in our knowledge of nature that have been made during the last four hundred years. But this method of work has also left us as legacy the habit of observing natural objects and processes in isolation, apart from their connection with the vast whole; of observing them in repose, not in motion; as constants, not as essentially variables; in their death, not in their life. And when this way of looking at things was transferred by Bacon and Locke from natural science to philosophy, it begot the narrow, metaphysical mode of thought peculiar to the last century.

To the metaphysician, things and their mental reflexes, ideas, are isolated, are to be considered one after the other and apart from each other, are objects of investigation fixed, rigid, given once for all. He thinks in absolutely irreconcilable antitheses. "His communication is 'yea, yea; nay, nay'; for whatsoever is more than these cometh of evil." For him a thing either exists or does not exist; a thing cannot at the same time be itself and something else. Positive and negative absolutely exclude one another; cause and effect stand in a rigid antithesis one to the other.

At first sight this mode of thinking seems to us very luminous, because it is that of so-called sound common sense. Only sound common sense, respectable fellow that he is, in the homely realm of his own four walls, has very wonderful adventures directly he ventures out into the wide world of research. And the metaphysical mode of thought, justifiable and necessary as it is in a number of domains whose extent varies according to the nature of the particular object of investigation, sooner or later reaches a limit, beyond which it becomes onesided, restricted, abstract, lost in insoluble contradictions. In the contemplation of individual things, it forgets the connection between them; in the contemplation of their existence, it forgets the beginning and end of that existence; of their repose, it forgets their motion. It cannot see the wood for the trees. For everyday purposes we know and can say, e.g., whether an animal is alive or not. But, upon closer inquiry, we find that this is, in many cases, a very complex question, as the jurists know very well. They have cudgelled their brains in vain to discover a rational limit beyond which the killing of the child in its mother's womb is murder. It is just as impossible to determine absolutely the moment of death, for physiology proves that death is not an instantaneous, momentary phenomenon, but a very protracted process.

In like manner, every organic being is every moment the same and not the same; every moment it assimilates matter supplied from without, and gets rid of other matter; every moment some cells of its body die and others build themselves anew; in a longer or shorter time the matter of its body is completely renewed, and is replaced by other molecules of matter, so that every organic being is always itself, and yet something other than itself.

Further, we find upon closer investigation that the two poles of an antithesis, positive and negative, e.g., are as inseparable as they are opposed, and that despite all their opposition, they mutually interpenetrate. And we find, in like manner, that cause and effect are conceptions which only hold good in their application to individual cases; but as soon as we consider the individual cases in their general connection with the universe as a whole, they run into each other, and they become confounded when we contemplate that universal action and reaction in which causes and effects are eternally changing places, so that what is effect here and now will be cause there and then, and vice versa.

None of these processes and modes of thought enters into the framework of metaphysical reasoning. Dialectics, on the other hand, comprehends things and their representations, in their essential connection, concatenation, motion, origin, and ending. Such processes as those mentioned above are, therefore, so many corroborations of its own method of procedure. . . .

This new German philosophy culminated in the Hegelian system. In this system—and herein is its great merit—for the first time the whole world, natural, historical, intellectual, is represented as a process, i.e., as in constant motion, change, transformation, development; and the attempt is made to trace out the internal connection that makes a continuous whole of all this movement and development. From this point of view the history of mankind no longer appeared as a wild whirl of senseless deeds of violence, all equally condemnable at the judgment seat of mature philosophic reason and which are best forgotten as quickly as possible, but as the process of evolution of man himself. It was now the task of the intellect to follow the gradual march of this process through all its devious ways, and to trace out the inner law running through all its apparently accidental phenomena.

That Hegel did not solve the problem is here immaterial. His epoch-making merit was that he propounded the problem. This problem is one that no single individual will ever be able to solve. Although Hegel was—with Saint-Simon— the most encyclopedic mind of his time, yet he was limited, first, by the necessarily limited extent of his own knowledge and, second, by the limited extent and depth of the knowledge and conceptions of his age. To these limits a third must be added. Hegel was an idealist. To him the thoughts within his brain were not the more or less abstract pictures of actual things and processes, but, conversely, things and their evolution were only the realized pictures of the "Idea," existing somewhere from eternity before the world was. This way of thinking turned everything upside down, and completely reversed the actual connection of things in the world. Correctly and ingeniously as many individual groups of facts were grasped by Hegel, yet, for the reasons just given, there is much that is botched, artificial, labored, in a word, wrong in point of detail. The Hegelian system, in itself, was a colossal miscarriage—but it was also the last of its kind. It was suffering, in fact, from an internal and incurable contradiction. Upon the one hand, its essential proposition was the conception that human history is a process of evolution, which, by its very nature, cannot find its intellectual final term in the discovery of any so-called absolute truth. But, on the other hand, it laid claim to being the very essence of the absolute truth. A system of natural and historical knowledge, embracing everything, and final for all time, is a contradiction to the fundamental law of dialectic reasoning. This law, indeed, by no means excludes, but, on the contrary, includes the idea that the systematic knowledge of the external universe can make giant strides from age to age.

The perception of the fundamental contradiction in German idealism led necessarily back to materialism, but, *nota bene,* not to the simply metaphysical, exclusively mechanical materialism of the eighteenth century. In contrast to the naively revolutionary, simple rejection of all previous history, modern materialism sees in the latter the process of evolution of humanity, it being its task to discover the laws of motion thereof. With the French of the eighteenth century, and with Hegel, the conception obtained of nature as a whole, moving in narrow circles, and immutable, with its eternal celestial bodies, as Newton, and unalterable organic species, as Linnaeus, taught. Modern materialism embraces the more recent discoveries of natural science, according to which nature also has its history in time, the celestial bodies, like the organic species that, under favorable conditions, people them, being born and perishing. And even if nature, as a whole, must still be said to move in recurrent cycles, these cycles assume infinitely larger dimensions. In both cases modern materialism is essentially dialectic, and no longer needs any philosophy standing above the other sciences. As soon as each special science is bound to make clear its position in the great totality of things and of our knowledge of things, a special science dealing with this totality is superfluous [or unnecessary]. That which still survives, independently, of all earlier philosophy is the science of thought and its laws—formal logic and dialectics. Everything else is subsumed in the positive science of nature and history.

Whilst, however, the revolution in the conception of nature could only be made in proportion to the corresponding positive materials furnished by research, already much earlier certain historical facts had occurred which led to a decisive change in the conception of history. In 1831, the first working-class rising took place in Lyons; between 1838 and 1842, the first national working-class movement, that of the English Chartists, reached its height. The class struggle between proletariat and bourgeoisie came to the front in the history of the most advanced countries in Europe, in proportion to the development, upon the one hand, of modern industry, upon the other, of the newly acquired political supremacy of the bourgeoisie. Facts more and more strenuously gave the lie to the teachings of bourgeois economy as to the identity of the interests of capital and labor, as to the universal harmony and universal prosperity that would be the consequence of unbridled competition. All these things could no longer be ignored, any more than the French and English socialism, which was their theoretical, though very imperfect, expression. But the old idealist conception of history, which was not yet dislodged, knew nothing of class struggles based upon economic interests, knew nothing of economic interests; production and all economic relations appeared in it only as incidental, subordinate elements in the "history of civilization."

The new facts made imperative a new examination of all past history. Then it was seen that *all* past history was the history of class struggles; that these warring classes of society are always the products of the modes of production and of exchange—in a word, of the *economic* conditions of their time; that the economic structure of society always furnishes the real basis, starting from which we can alone work out the ultimate explanation of the whole superstructure of juridical and political institutions as well as of the religious, philosophical, and other ideas of a given historical period. But now idealism was driven from its last refuge, the philosophy of history; now a materialistic treatment of history was propounded, and a method found of explaining man's "knowing" by his "being," instead of, as heretofore, his "being" by his "knowing."

But the socialism of earlier days was as incompatible with this materialistic conception as the conception of nature of the French materialists was with dialectics and modern natural science. The socialism of earlier days certainly criticized the existing capitalistic mode of production and its consequences. But it could not explain them, and, therefore, could not get the mastery of them. It could only simply reject them as bad. The more strongly this earlier socialism denounced the exploitation of the working class, inevitable under capitalism, the less able was it clearly to show in what this exploitation consisted and how it arose. But for this it was necessary—(1) to present the capitalistic method of production in its historical connection and its inevitableness during a particular historical period, and therefore, also, to present its inevitable downfall; and (2) to lay bare its essential character, which was still a secret, as its critics had hitherto attacked its evil consequences rather than the process of the thing itself. This was done by the discovery of *surplus value*. It was shown that the appropriation of unpaid labor is the basis of the capitalist mode of production and of the exploitation of the worker that occurs under it; that even if the capitalist buys the labor-power of his laborer at its full value as a commodity on the market, he yet extracts more value from it than he paid for; and that in the ultimate analysis this surplus value forms those sums of value from which are heaped up the constantly increasing masses of capital in the hands of the possessing classes. The genesis of capitalist production and the production of capital were both explained.

These two great discoveries, the materialistic conception of history and the revelation of the secret of capitalistic production through surplus value, we owe to *Marx*. With these discoveries socialism became a science. The next thing was to work out all its details. . . .

MARX: THE FUTURE OF COMMUNISM

*Marx never fully stated the details of the future communist
society, but he came closest to doing so in 1875, in a caustic
review of the program adopted by his followers in the new
German Social-Democratic Party. The "lower" and "higher"
stages of communism envisaged by Marx were later given the
respective labels "socialism" and "communism" by Lenin. The
Soviet Union now claims to have completed "socialism," left
the "dictatorship of the proletariat" behind, and started the
"transition to communism."*

CRITIQUE OF THE GOTHA PROGRAM

. . . Within the cooperative society based on common ownership of the means of production, the producers do not
exchange their products; just as little does the labor employed on the products appear here *as the value* of these
products, as a material quality possessed by them, since
now, in contrast to capitalist society, individual labor no
longer exists in an indirect fashion but directly as a com-
ponent part of the total labor. The phrase "proceeds of
labor," objectionable even today on account of its am-
biguity, thus loses all meaning.

What we have to deal with here is a communist society,
not as it has *developed* on its own foundations, but, on the
contrary, as it *emerges* from capitalist society; which is thus
in every respect, economically, morally and intellectually,
still stamped with the birthmarks of the old society from
whose womb it emerges. Accordingly the individual producer receives back from society—after the deductions have
been made—exactly what he gives to it. What he has given
to it is his individual amount of labor. For example, the
social working day consists of the sum of the individual
labor hours; the individual labor time of the individual
producer is the part of the social labor day contributed
by him, his share in it. He receives a certificate from society that he has furnished such and such an amount of

From Karl Marx, *Critique of the Gotha Program*, in Marx, *Selected Works*
(New York, International Publishers, n.d.), Vol. II, pp. 563-566, 577.

labor (after deducting his labor for the common fund), and with this certificate he draws from the social stock of means of consumption as much as costs the same amount of labor. The same amount of labor which he has given to society in one form, he receives back in another.

Here obviously the same principle prevails as that which regulates the exchange of commodities, as far as this is exchange of equal values. Content and form are changed, because under the altered circumstances no one can give anything except his labor, and because, on the other hand, nothing can pass into the ownership of individuals except individual means of consumption. But, as far as the distribution of the latter among the individual producers is concerned, the same principle prevails as in the exchange of commodity equivalents, so much labor in one form is exchanged for an equal amount of labor in another form.

Hence, *equal right* here is still in principle—*bourgeois right*, although principle and practice are no longer in conflict, while the exchange of equivalents in commodity exchange only exists on the *average* and not in the individual case.

In spite of this advance, this *equal right* is still stigmatized by a bourgeois limitation. The right of the producers is *proportional* to the labor they supply; the equality consists in the fact that measurement is made with an *equal standard*, labor.

But one man is superior to another physically or mentally and so supplies more labor in the same time, or can labor for a longer time; and labor, to serve as a measure, must be defined by its duration or intensity, otherwise it ceases to be a standard of measurement. This *equal* right is an unequal right for unequal labor. It recognizes no class differences, because everyone is only a worker like everyone else; but it tacitly recognizes unequal individual endowment and thus productive capacity as natural privileges. *It is therefore a right of inequality in its content, like every right.* Right by its very nature can only consist in the application of an equal standard; but unequal individuals (and they would not be different individuals if they were not unequal) are only measurable by an equal standard in so far as they are brought under an equal point of view, are taken from one *definite* side only, *e.g.*, in the present case are regarded *only as workers*, and nothing more seen in them, everything else being ignored. Further, one worker is married, another not; one has more children than another and so on and so forth. Thus with an equal output, and hence an equal share in the social consumption fund, one will in fact receive more than another, one will be richer than another, and so on. To avoid all these defects, right instead of being equal would have to be unequal.

But these defects are inevitable in the first phase of communist society as it is when it has just emerged after prolonged birthpangs from capitalist society. Right can never be higher than the economic structure of society and the cultural development thereby determined.

In a higher phase of communist society, after the enslaving subordination of individuals under division of labor, and therewith also the antithesis between mental and physical labor, has vanished, after labor has become not merely a means to live but has become itself the primary necessity of life, after the productive forces have also increased with the all-around development of the individual, and all the springs of cooperative wealth flow more abundantly—only then can the narrow horizon of bourgeois right be fully left behind and society inscribe on its banners: from each according to his ability, to each according to his needs. . . .

"Present-day society" is capitalist society, which exists in all civilized countries, more or less free from medieval admixture, more or less modified by the special historical development of each country and more or less developed. On the other hand, the "present-day state" changes with a country's frontier. It is different in the Prusso-German empire from what it is in Switzerland, it is different in England from what it is in the United States. "*The* present-day state" is therefore a fiction.

Nevertheless, the different states of the different civilized countries, in spite of their manifold diversity of form, all have this in common: that they are based on modern bourgeois society, only one more or less capitalistically developed. They have, therefore, also certain essential features in common. In this sense it is possible to speak of the "present-day state," in contrast to the future in which its present root, bourgeois society, will have died away.

The question then arises: what transformation will the state undergo in communist society? In other words, what social functions will remain in existence there that are analogous to the present functions of the state? This question can only be answered scientifically and one does not get a flea-hop nearer to the problem by a thousandfold combination of the word people with the word state.

Between capitalist and communist society lies the period of the revolutionary transformation of the one into the other. There corresponds to this also a political transition period in which the state can be nothing but *the revolutionary dictatorship of the proletariat*.

ENGELS: REVOLUTION BY BALLOT

Between the 1860's and the 1890's, the right to vote became a reality for the working class in most European countries, as it had earlier in the United States. Marx and Engels welcomed this development as a path to revolution without violence. After Marx died and shortly before his own death, Engels elaborated this view in a new introduction to Marx's book on the French Revolution of 1848.

Introduction to

THE CLASS STRUGGLES IN FRANCE

. . . The war of 1870–71 and the defeat of the Commune had transferred the center of gravity of the European workers' movement for the time being from France to Germany, as Marx foretold. In France it naturally took years to recover from the bloodletting of May 1871. In Germany, on the other hand, where industry was, in addition, furthered (in positively hothouse fashion) by the blessing of the French milliards and developed more and more quickly, Social-Democracy experienced a much more rapid and enduring growth. Thanks to the understanding with which the German workers made use of the universal suffrage introduced in 1866 the astonishing growth of the Party is made plain to all the world by incontestable figures: 1871, 102,000; 1874, 352,000; 1877, 493,000 Social-Democratic votes. Then came recognition of this advance by high authority in the shape of the Anti-Socialist Law: the Party was temporarily disrupted; the number of votes sank to 312,000 in 1881. But that was quickly overcome, and then, though oppressed by the Exceptional Law, without press, without external organization and without the right of combination or meeting, the rapid expansion really began: 1884, 550,000; 1887, 763,000; 1890, 1,427,-000 votes. Then the hand of the state was paralyzed. The Anti-Socialist Law disappeared; socialist votes rose to 1,-

From Friedrich Engels, 1895 introduction to Marx's *The Class Struggles in France, 1848-1850*, in Marx, *Selected Works* (New York, International Publishers, n.d.), Vol. II, pp. 180-181, 183-184, 188-189.

787,000, over a quarter of all the votes cast. The government and the ruling classes had exhausted all their expedients—uselessly, to no purpose, and without success. The tangible proofs of their impotence, which the authorities, from night watchman to the imperial chancellor, had had to accept—and that from the despised workers—these proofs were counted in millions. The state was at the end of its Latin, the workers only at the beginning of theirs.

But the German workers rendered a second great service to their cause in addition to the first, which they performed by their mere existence as the strongest, best disciplined and most rapidly growing Socialist Party. They supplied their comrades of all countries with a new weapon, and one of the sharpest, when they showed them how to use universal suffrage. . . .

With this successful utilization of universal suffrage, an entirely new mode of proletarian struggle came into force, and this quickly developed further. It was found that the state institutions, in which the rule of the bourgeoisie is organized, offer still further opportunities for the working class to fight these very state institutions. They took part in elections to individual Diets, to municipal councils and to industrial courts; they contested with the bourgeoisie for every post in the occupation of which a sufficient part of the proletariat had a say. And so it happened that the bourgeoisie and the government came to be much more afraid of the legal than of the illegal action of the Workers' Party, of the results of elections than of those of rebellion.

For here, too, the conditions of the struggle had essentially changed. Rebellion in the old style, the street fight with barricades, which up to 1848 gave everywhere the final decision, was to a considerable extent obsolete.

Let us have no illusions about it: a real victory of an insurrection over the military in street fighting, a victory as between two armies, is one of the rarest exceptions. But the insurgents, also, counted on it just as rarely. For them it was solely a question of making the troops yield to moral influences, which, in a fight between the armies of two warring countries do not come into play at all, or do so to a much less degree. If they succeed in this, then the troops fail to act, or the commanding officers lose their heads, and the insurrection wins. If they do not succeed in this, then, even where the military are in the minority, the superiority of better equipment and training, of unified leadership, of the planned employment of the military forces and of discipline makes itself felt. The most that the insurrection can achieve in actual tactical practice is the correct construction and defense of a single barricade. Mutual support; the disposition and employment of reserves; in short, the cooperation and harmonious working of the individual detachments, indispensable even for the defense of one quarter of the town, not to speak of the whole of a large town, are at best defective, and mostly not attainable at all; concentration of the military forces at a decisive point is of course impossible. Hence the passive defense is the prevailing form of fight: the attack will rise here and there, but only by way of exception, to occasional advances and flank assaults; as a rule, however, it will be limited to occupation of the positions abandoned by the retreating troops. In addition, the military have, on their side, the disposal of artillery and fully equipped corps of skilled engineers, resources of war which, in nearly every case, the insurgents entirely lack. . . .

But whatever may happen in other countries, German Social-Democracy has a special situation and therewith, at least in the first instance, a special task. The two million voters whom it sends to the ballot box, together with the young men and women who stand behind them as nonvoters, form the most numerous, most compact mass, the decisive *"shock force"* of the international proletarian army. This mass already supplies over a fourth of the recorded votes; and as the by-elections to the Reichstag, the diet elections in individual states, the municipal council and industrial court elections demonstrate, it increases uninterruptedly. Its growth proceeds as spontaneously, as steadily, as irresistibly, and at the same time as tranquilly as a natural process. All government intervention has proved powerless against it. We can count even today on two and a half million voters. If it continues in this fashion, by the end of the century we shall conquer the greater part of the middle section of society, petty bourgeois and small peasants, and grow into the decisive power in the land, before which all other powers will have to bow, whether they like it or not. To keep this growth going without interruption until of itself it gets beyond the control of the ruling governmental system [*not to fritter away this daily increasing shock force in advance guard fighting, but to keep it intact until the day of the decision*]* that is our main task. And there is only one means by which the steady rise of the socialist fighting forces in Germany could be momentarily halted, and even thrown back for some time: a clash on a big scale with the military, a bloodbath like that of 1871 in Paris. In the long run that would also be overcome. To shoot out of the world a party which numbers millions—all the magazine rifles of Europe and America are not enough for this. But the normal development would be impeded [*the shock force would, perhaps, not be available at the critical moment*], *the decisive struggle* would be delayed, protracted and attended by heavy sacrifices.

The irony of world history turns everything upside down. We, the "revolutionaries," the "rebels"—we are thriving far better on legal methods than on illegal methods and revolt. The parties of order, as they call themselves, are perishing under the legal conditions created by themselves. They cry despairingly with Odilon Barrot: *la légalité nous tue*, legality is the death of us; whereas we, under this legality, get firm muscles and rosy cheeks and look like eternal life. And if we are not so crazy as to let ourselves be driven into street fighting in order to please them, then nothing else is finally left for them but themselves to break through this legality so fatal to them.

---

* The bracketed phrases were cut from the originally published version of the introduction, and restored by the Soviet editor. [Ed.]

BERNSTEIN: SOCIALISM AND DEMOCRACY

Eduard Bernstein (1850–1932) was the leader of the "revisionist" wing of the German Social-Democratic Party. He believed Marxist theory should be thoroughly and frankly revised to take account of the possibility of democratic evolution toward socialism. Bernstein was opposed both by the revolutionary radicals who later became Communists, and by the "orthodox" Marxists who kept to the old theory of revolution even though they had accepted democratic methods. After the Russian Revolution, most anti-Communist Socialists accepted Bernstein's evolutionary approach.

EVOLUTIONARY SOCIALISM

What is the principle of democracy?

The answer to this appears very simple. At first one would think it settled by the definition "government by the people." But even a little consideration tells us that by that only quite a superficial, purely formal definition is given, whilst nearly all who use the word democracy today understand by it more than a mere form of government. We shall come much nearer to the definition if we express ourselves negatively, and define democracy as an absence of class government, as the indication of a social condition where a political privilege belongs to no one class as opposed to the whole community. By that the explanation is already given as to why a monopolist corporation is in principle anti-democratic. This negative definition has, besides, the advantage that it gives less room than the phrase "government by the people" to the idea of the oppression of the individual by the majority which is absolutely repugnant to the modern mind. To-day we find the oppression of the minority by the majority "undemocratic," although it was originally held to be quite consistent with government by the people. The idea of democracy includes, in the conception of the present day, a notion of justice— an equality of rights for all members of the community,

From Eduard Bernstein, *Evolutionary Socialism* (English translation, New York, Huebsch, 1909), pp. 141-147, 166-167, 206-207, 210-211.

and in that principle the rule of the majority, to which in every concrete case the rule of the people extends, finds its limits. The more it is adopted and governs the general consciousness, the more will democracy be equal in meaning to the highest possible degree of freedom for all.

Democracy is in principle the suppression of class government, though it is not yet the actual suppression of classes. They speak of the conservative character of the democracy, and to a certain degree rightly. Absolutism, or semi-absolutism, deceives its supporters as well as its opponents as to the extent of their power. Therefore in countries where it obtains, or where its traditions still exist, we have flitting plans, exaggerated language, zigzag politics, fear of revolution, hope in oppression. In a democracy the parties, and the classes standing behind them, soon learn to know the limits of their power, and to undertake each time only as much as they can reasonably hope to carry through under the existing circumstances. Even if they make their demands rather higher than they seriously mean in order to give way in the unavoidable compromise —and democracy is the high school of compromise—they must still be moderate. The right to vote in a democracy makes its members virtually partners in the community, and this virtual partnership must in the end lead to real partnership. With a working class undeveloped in numbers and culture the general right to vote may long appear as the right to choose "the butcher"; with the growing number and knowledge of the workers it is changed, however, into the implement by which to transform the representatives of the people from masters into real servants of the people. . . .

. . . Phrases which were composed in a time when the political privilege of property ruled all over Europe, and which under these circumstances were explanatory, and to a certain degree also justified, but which to-day are only a dead weight, are treated with such reverence as though the progress of the movement depended on them and not on the understanding of what can be done, and what should be done. Is there any sense, for example, in maintaining the phrase of the "dictatorship of the proletariat" at a time when in all possible places representatives of social democracy have placed themselves practically in the arena of Parliamentary work, have declared for the proportional representation of the people, and for direct legislation—all of which is inconsistent with a dictatorship.

The phrase is to-day so antiquated that it is only to be reconciled with reality by stripping the word dictatorship of its actual meaning and attaching to it some kind of weakened interpretation. The whole practical activity of social democracy is directed towards creating circumstances and conditions which shall render possible and secure a transition (free from convulsive outbursts) of the modern social order into a higher one. From the consciousness of being the pioneers of a higher civilization, its adherents are ever creating fresh inspiration and zeal. In this rests also, finally, the moral justification of the socialist expropriation towards which they aspire. But the "dictatorship of the classes" belongs to a lower civilization, and apart from the question of the expediency and practicability of the thing, it is only to be looked upon as a reversion, as political atavism. If the thought is aroused that the transition from a capitalist to a socialist society must necessarily be accomplished by means of the development of forms of an age which did not know at all, or only in quite an imperfect form, the present methods of the initiating and carrying of laws, and which was without the organs fit for the purpose, reaction will set in. . . .

. . . Democracy is a condition of socialism to a much greater degree than is usually assumed, *i.e.*, it is not only the means but also the substance. Without a certain amount of democratic institutions or traditions, the socialist doctrine of the present time would not indeed be possible. There would, indeed, be a workers' movement, but no social democracy. The modern socialist movement—and also its theoretic explanation—is actually the product of the influence of the great French Revolution and of the conceptions of right which through it gained general acceptance in the wage and labor movement. The movement itself would exist without them as, without and before them, a communism of the people was linked to primitive Christianity.

But this communism of the people was very indefinite and half mythical, and the workers' movement would lack inner cohesion without the foundation of those organizations and conceptions of law which, at least to a great part, necessarily accompany capitalist evolution. A working class politically without rights, grown up in superstition and with deficient education, will certainly revolt sometimes and join in small conspiracies, but never develop a socialist movement. It requires a certain breadth of vision and a fairly well developed consciousness of rights to make a socialist out of a workman who is accidentally a revolter. Political rights and education stand indeed everywhere in a prominent position in the socialist program of action. . . .

Unfortunately for the scientific socialism of Plekhanov, the Marxist propositions on the hopelessness of the position of the worker have been upset in a book which bears the title, *Capital: A Criticism of Political Economy.* There we read of the "physical and moral regeneration" of the textile workers in Lancashire through the Factory Law of 1847, which "struck the feeblest eye." A bourgeois republic was not even necessary to bring about a certain improvement in the situation of a large section of workers! In the same book we read that the society of to-day is no firm crystal, but an organism capable of change and constantly engaged in a process of change, that also in the treatment of economic questions on the part of the official representatives of this society an "improvement was unmistakable." Further that the author had devoted so large a space in his book to the results of the English Factory Laws in order to spur the Continent to imitate them and thus to work so that the process of transforming society may be accomplished in ever more humane forms. All of which signifies not hopelessness but capability of improvement in the condition of the worker. And, as since 1866, when this was written, the legislation depicted has not grown weaker but has been improved, made more general, and has been supplemented by laws and organizations working in the same direction, there can be no more doubt today than formerly of the hopefulness of the position of the worker. If to state such facts means following the "immortal Bastiat," then among the first ranks of these followers is—Karl Marx. . . .

. . . The general sympathy with the strivings for emancipation of the working classes does not in itself stand in the way of the scientific method. But, as Marx approaches a point when that final aim enters seriously into the question, he becomes uncertain and unreliable. Such contradictions then appear as were shown in the book under consideration, for instance in the section on the movement of incomes in modern society. It thus appears that this great scientific spirit was, in the end, a slave to a doctrine. To express it figuratively, he has raised a mighty building within the framework of a scaffolding he found existing, and in its erection he kept strictly to the laws of scientific architecture as long as they did not collide with the conditions which the construction of the scaffolding prescribed, but he neglected or evaded them when the scaffolding did not allow of their observance. Where the scaffolding put limits in the way of the building, instead of destroying the scaffolding, he changed the building itself at the cost of its right proportions and so made it all the more dependent on the scaffolding. Was it the consciousness of this irrational relation which caused him continually to pass from completing his work to amending special parts of it? However that may be, my conviction is that wherever that dualism shows itself the scaffolding must fall if the building is to grow in its right proportions. In the latter, and not in the former, is found what is worthy to live in Marx.

PART TWO

RUSSIAN COMMUNISM

Communism as a political movement of worldwide significance dates from the Russian Revolution of 1917. This event forced Marxists around the world to choose between the Western democratic version of socialism and the revolutionary course proclaimed by the Russian Bolsheviks. Communism, representing the latter alternative, is therefore distinctly Russian in its origin, the child of the revolutionary upheaval in Russia and of the political ideas of Lenin.

Communism has drawn heavily on the doctrines of Marx and Engels, perhaps more for the purpose of propaganda and self-justification than for actual guidance. In 1918, shortly after the seizure of power, Lenin's Bolshevik Party took the name "Communist Party," in order to recall the 1848 radicalism of Marx and Engels. However, progress in the Soviet Union toward the social goal of true "communism" has been largely fictional. The basic features distinguishing the modern Communist movement are not to be found in its name or in its doctrinal heritage (apart from the professed faith in Marxism), but in the tactical formulations and organizational methods that make up "Leninism."

Marxism first became influential in Russia in the 1890's, thanks to the writings of Georgi Plekhanov. The ground was already prepared among the Russian intellectuals by a long tradition of native revolutionary socialist thought, which went back to Alexander Herzen, writing during the 1840's and 1850's. Though Russia was hardly ripe for the kind of proletarian revolution Marxism predicted, the theory nevertheless found a ready response among those members of the intelligentsia who presumed to speak for the growing class of industrial workers. Lenin's contribution—most directly in his 1902 pamphlet, *What Is to Be*

Done?—was to graft the foliage of Marxian theory onto the roots of Russian revolutionary thought. His doctrine of revolution caused the newly established Marxist party, the "Russian Social-Democratic Workers Party," to split into two factions, the more moderate and democratic Mensheviks and Lenin's extremist Bolsheviks.

The victory of the Bolsheviks in the Revolution of 1917 precipitated a similar split among Marxists all over the world, between the democratic Socialists, who remained with the old Second International, and the radicals, who joined the new Third or Communist International. The cardinal principles of the new movement were violent revolution, the disciplined party, and loyalty to the Russian Revolution. These have remained the essential features of contemporary international Communism, despite the development, under the successive dictatorships of Stalin and Khrushchev, of a bureaucratic industrial society.

HERZEN: RUSSIAN SOCIALISM

Alexander Herzen (1812–1870) was a member of the upper-class Russian intelligentsia, who left Russia for France and England in order to be free to criticize the Tsarist system. Herzen believed that Russia had the power to lead an international socialist revolution, thanks to the Russian tradition of the communal peasant village. He spelled out this argument in 1851 to protest the view of the French historian Michelet that Russia was simply a menace to civilization.

Herzen's philosophy was the primary intellectual inspiration for the movement of Russian Populism in the later nineteenth century. Its assumptions strongly colored the interpretations of Marxism by Lenin, Trotsky, and Stalin.

THE RUSSIAN PEOPLE AND SOCIALISM

. . . It is time that Europe was made to realize that nowadays speaking about Russia is no longer a matter of speaking about a country that is absent, distant, mute.

For we are present, we who have left our country only so that free Russian speech may be heard in Europe. And we hold it our duty to speak out when a man, who quite rightly enjoys such immense authority, tells us that "he knows—that he swears to it—that he can prove that Russia doesn't exist, that the Russians are not human, that they are devoid of all moral sense."

Do you mean by this official Russia, the Empire of façades, the Byzantine-German government?* If so, you are right. We agree in advance with everything you say. We feel no need to rush into the breach. The Russian government has enough agents in the Paris press to provide a permanent stream of eloquent justifications of its doings.

But it is not only official society that you deal with in your book. You have taken the problem and have gone to its very roots. You have written about the People.

From Alexander Herzen, "The Russian People and Socialism—An Open Letter to Jules Michelet," in Herzen, *From The Other Shore* and *The Russian People and Socialism* (London, Library of Ideas, 1956), pp. 165-167, 169, 176-178, 180-181, 188-190.
* The allusion is to the medieval Byzantine influence and Westernization since Peter the Great. [Ed.]

The poor Russian people has no one of its own to raise
a voice in its defense. I ask you, then—can we, in such circumstances, without gross cowardice, stay silent?

The Russian people, Sir, does not exist. It lives. It is not
even very old. It is very young. Sometimes (it is true) one
dies young, before one has had time to live. It can happen,
but not in the ordinary run of events.

For the Russian people the past is dark: the present is
terrible: but for all that, it lays some claim to the future,
it *has no belief* in its present condition. It has the audacity
to hope: and it hopes all the more, since it possesses so
little. . . .

. . . Europe is approaching a terrible cataclysm. The world
of the Middle Ages has come to an end. The world of
feudalism is expiring. The religious and political revolutions are petering out under the weight of their own complete impotence. They have great achievements to their
credit, but they have failed to complete their tasks. They
have stripped Throne and Altar of the prestige they once
enjoyed, but they have not established the era of freedom.
They have lit new desires in the hearts of men but they
have not provided ways of satisfying them. Parliamentari-
anism, Protestantism—these are mere prevarications, temporary measures, attempts to stave off the flood, which can
arrest only for a short while the process of death and re-
birth. The time for them has passed. Since 1848 it has
become apparent that no amount of delving into Roman
law, of barren casuistry, of thin philosophic deism, of sterile
religious rationalism can hold back society from fulfilling
its destiny.

The storm draws near. There can no longer be doubt
about it; on this point revolutionaries and reactionaries
agree. Men's minds are unbalanced: a serious question, a
question of life and death, lies heavy on their hearts. Men
grow worried, disturbed. They ask themselves, is it still
possible for Europe, that hoary Proteus, that decaying organism, to find within itself the strength to bring about
its own recovery? And having asked the question, they
dread the answer. They tremble with suspense. . . .

Turning away from this chaos, from the writhings of insanity and the tears and pains of childbirth, turning away from this world as it falls into rotting pieces by the cradle's side, men's eyes turn involuntarily to the East.

There, like some dark mountain emerging from the mists, may be discerned the unfriendly, menacing contours of an empire: it seems to advance upon one like an avalanche— or like an impatient heir anxious to hurry on the last protracted moments of his dying benefactor.

This empire, totally unknown two centuries ago, has suddenly burst in upon the world, as if by sheer force, and with no invitation, with no real right, has taken its place at the council table of the sovereigns of Europe, and has peremptorily demanded its share of the booty, although this was won without its assistance.

No one has yet dared oppose its claims to interfere in the affairs of Europe. . . .

. . . The majority of the Slav peoples have never been subjugated by a conquering race. For them submision has, on the whole, been confined to the recognition of an overlord and to the payment of some form of tribute. Such, for instance, was the Mongol rule in Russia. As a result, the Slavs have managed to preserve for some hundreds of years their nationality, their way of life and their language.

The great question then is this: Is it reasonable to expect that Russia will be the nucleus of this crystallization, the center towards which the Slav world will gravitate? a question we should ask realizing that so far she is the only section of that great race to be even provisionally organized into a State; and that there she stands, powerful, independent, armed with two swords, the one pointed against Germany, the other threatening Turkey. There could be no doubt at all about the answer to this question, if the Petersburg government had the faintest inkling of its national vocation, if any humane idea of any sort whatever could even once penetrate that gloomy and dull-witted despotism. But, as things are, how can anyone of any integrity or decency dare suggest to the western Slavs that they should ally themselves with an empire which lives in

a permanent state of siege and where the scepter is wielded
like a truncheon in the hands of a flogging corporal.

The idea of a union based on the principles of freedom
must not be confused with Imperial Panslavism, as it has
been expounded in the past by misguided or corrupted
men.

At this point, logic compels us to raise what is really the
most serious, the most genuine question of all:

If we suppose that the Slav world has prospects of some
more developed form of life in the future, then, which of
all its somewhat embryonic elements is the most advanced,
which gives the best ground for such hopes? If the Slavs
are right in believing that their hour has come, then this
element must necessarily be that which is in line with
revolutionary ideas in Europe.

You have suggested which this element might be, you
have touched upon it, but then you let it elude your grasp
while you brushed away a tear of compassion for the fate
of Poland.

You maintain that "the basis of the life of the Russian
people is COMMUNISM": you assert that "its strength is
founded on a form of agrarian law, on perpetual sub-
division of the land."

What a terrible MENE TEKEL have you pronounced. . . .
Communism as a basis of life! Sub-division of the land as
a source of strength! How is it, Sir, that you were not
frightened by your own words?

Should we not pause here for reflection, and not leave
the question until we have convinced you whether this is in
fact the truth or whether it is pure fantasy?

As though there were any other real subjects of inquiry,
any other serious questions for the nineteenth century than
this question of communism and land division!

Carried away by indignation, you proceed: 'What they
(the Russians) lack is that essential human attribute, the
moral faculty, the sense of right and wrong. Truth and
justice mean nothing to them. Mention these words to them
—and they are mute, they smile at you, they don't understand what you are talking about.' Who are these Russians

with whom you have spoken? And what notions of Justice
and Truth are they that the Russians cannot understand?
For in a genuinely revolutionary age, it is not enough
simply to mention the words *truth* and *justice*. For these
words no longer need have a meaning that is fixed and un-
ambiguous for all of us alike.

The Justice and Truth of the old Europe are the injustice
and falsehood of the Europe that is being born. . . .

. . . The Russian peasant who has, as you have rightly
observed, a strong aversion to every form of landed property, who is improvident and indolent by temperament, has
gradually and imperceptibly found himself caught up in
the tentacles of the German [i.e., modern] bureaucracy
and the feudal power. He has submitted to this degrading
yoke with, I agree, the passivity of despair, but he has never
believed either in the authority of his lord, or in the justice
of the courts, or in the equity of the administration. For
almost two hundred years, his whole life has been one
long, dumb, passive opposition to the existing order of
things: he has endured oppression, he has groaned under
it: but he has never accepted anything that goes on outside the life of the rural commune.

The idea of the Tsar still enjoys some considerable prestige in the mind of the peasant. But it is not the actual
Tsar Nicholas whom he adores, it is rather an abstract idea,
a myth, a kind of Providence, an Avenger of evils, an
embodiment of justice in the popular imagination.

Apart from the Tsar, only the clergy are capable of having any moral influence on Orthodox Russia. The higher
clergy are the sole representatives of ancient Russia within
the administration. The clergy have never shaved off their
beards, and through this very fact have remained on the
side of the people. The people have complete faith in anything they are told by a monk. However, the monks and
the higher clergy, for all their talk about being dedicated
to matters not of this world, are almost entirely indifferent
to the people. The village priest has lost all influence on
account of his greed, his drunkenness, and his close associa-

tion with the police. Here again, it is not the man but the idea that the people respect.

As for the Dissenters, they hate both the Tsar and the village priest, both the man and the idea.

Apart from the Tsar and the clergy, all the other elements within society and the administration are utterly alien and ultimately hostile to the people. The peasant is, quite literally, outside the law: the law contrives to offer him absolutely no protection whatsoever, and his only share in the existing order of things is confined to the payment of the double tribute which grinds him down: the tribute of blood and the tribute of sweat. So, spurned on all sides, he comes to feel that the government is not for him but against him, that the single aim of the administration and the nobility is to extort from him as much work and as much money as possible. Realizing this and blessed with a certain shrewd, cunning intelligence he manages to deceive all of them all the time. . . .

. . . The party of movement, of progress, demands the emancipation of the peasants; and its members are ready to set an example by sacrificing their own rights. The Tsar is in a state of permanent indecision, and has lost the power of all real thought: he wants emancipation, and yet does all he can to prevent it.

He has come to see that the emancipation of the peasant is tantamount to the emancipation of the land: and that the emancipation of the land would in turn usher in a social revolution and would make rural communism sacrosanct. To evade this question of emancipation is certainly impossible: to postpone it until the reign of his successor would be easier but cowardly, and the time gained would really be no better than time spent in a wretched posting-station waiting for fresh horses.

From all this you can see what a blessing it is for Russia that the rural commune has never been broken up, that private ownership has never replaced the property of the commune: how fortunate it is for the Russian people that they have remained outside all political movements, and, for that matter, outside European civilization, which would undoubtedly have sapped the life of the commune, and which to-day in Socialism has achieved its own negation.

Europe, as I have pointed out elsewhere, has never solved the antinomy of the State and the individual, but it has stated the problem. Russia approaches the same problem from a quite different direction, but it has had no greater success in finding a solution to it. It is then in the shadow of this problem that we find the source of our equality.

Europe, now on the point of taking the first step forward in a social revolution, is confronted by a country that can provide an actual instance of an attempt—a crude, barbaric attempt perhaps, but still an attempt of a sort—in the direction of the division of the land amongst those who work it. And observe that this lesson is provided not by civilized Russia but by the people themselves in their daily lives. We Russians who have absorbed European civilization cannot hope to be more than a means to an end—the yeast in the leavening—a bridge between the Russian people and revolutionary Europe. The future of Russia lies with the *moujik* [the peasant], just as the regeneration of France lies with the worker.

PLEKHANOV: THE APPLICATION OF MARXISM TO RUSSIA

Georgi Plekhanov (1857–1918) took part in the Russian Populist movement of the 1870's, and then fled to Switzerland, where he became a follower of Marx and Engels. The object of his writings was to convince Russian revolutionaries that Russia had to pass through capitalism before a proletarian revolution could be successfully attempted. Plekhanov first expounded this view at length in 1885, in a polemic against Lev Tikhomirov of the terrorist "People's Will" group.

OUR DIFFERENCES

. . . Will Russia go through the school of capitalism? We shall answer without any hesitation: why should she not finish the school she has *already begun?*

All the newest, and therefore most influential, trends of social life, all the more remarkable facts in the fields of production and exchange have one meaning which can be neither doubted nor disputed: not only are they clearing the road for capitalism, they themselves are necessary and highly important moments in its development. *Capitalism is favored* by the whole dynamics of our social life, all the forces that develop with the movement of the social machine and in their turn determine the direction and speed of that movement. *Against capitalism* are only the more or less doubtful interests of a certain portion of the peasantry and also that force of inertia which occasionally is felt so painfully by educated people in every backward, agrarian country. But the peasants are not strong enough to defend their real interests; on the other hand, they are often not interested enough to defend with energy the old principles of communal life. The main stream of Russian capital is as yet not great; there are still not many places in Russia where the relations of the hirer of labor to the laborer correspond entirely to the generally current idea of the relations between labor and capital in capitalist society; but towards this stream are converging from all directions such

From Georgi Plekhanov, *Our Differences,* in Plekhanov, *Selected Philosophical Works* (Moscow, Foreign Languages Publishing House, n.d.), Vol. I, pp. 309-310, 369-374, 377-380.

a number of rivers, big and small, of rivulets and stream-
lets, that the total volume of water flowing towards it is
enormous, and there can be no doubt that the stream will
grow quickly and vigorously. For it cannot be stopped, and
still less can it be dried up; all that remains possible is
to reguate its flow if we do not want it to bring us nothing
but harm and if we are not abandoning hope of submitting
at least partly the elemental force of nature to the rational
activity of man.

But what must we Russian socialists do in this case, we
who are accustomed to thinking that our country has some
charter of exceptionalism granted to it by history for ser-
vices which nobody, however, is aware of?

It is not difficult to answer that question.

All laws of social development which are not understood
work with the irresistible force and blind harshness of laws
of nature. But to discover this or that law of nature or of
social development means, firstly, to be able to avoid clash-
ing with it and, consequently, expending one's efforts in
vain, and, secondly, to be able to regulate its application in
such a manner as to draw profit from it. This general idea
applies entirely to the particular case we are interested in.
We must utilize the social and economic upheaval which
is proceeding in Russia for the benefit of the revolution
and the working population. The highly important circum-
stance that the socialist movement in our country began
when capitalism was only in the embryo must not be lost
on us. . . .

The time of the "socialist organization in the sphere of
home exchange" will not come until it is possible to remove all the contradictions that have been pointed out.
And that will be possible only when the *labor of each individual person assumes a social character*. That can be the
case only when the whole of the social production mechanism constitutes a single planned entity. . . .

What will happen if the revolutionaries [seize power
prematurely] . . . ?

What will happen then? Oh, then there will be a most

disgraceful fiasco for the Russian socialist party! It will be
obliged to undertake an "organization" for which it has
neither the necessary strength nor the requisite understanding. Everything will combine to defeat it: its own unpre-
paredness, the hostility of the higher estates and the rural
bourgeoisie, the people's indifference to its *organizational*
plans and the underdeveloped state of our economic relations in general. The Russian socialist party will provide
but a new historical example corroborating the thought expressed by Engels in connection with the Peasant War in
Germany. "The worst thing that can befall a leader of an
extreme party is to be compelled to take over a government in an epoch when the movement is not yet ripe for
the domination of the class which he represents, and for
the realization of the measures which that domination implies. What he *can* do depends not upon his will but upon
the degree of contradiction between the various classes,
and upon the level of development of the material means
of existence, of the conditions of production and commerce
upon which class contradictions always repose. What he
ought to do, what his party demands of him, again depends
not upon him or the stage of development of the class
struggle and its conditions. He is bound to the doctrines
and demands hitherto propounded which, again, do not
proceed from the class relations *of the moment,** or from
the more or less *accidental** level of production and commerce, but from his more or less penetrating insight into
the general result of the social and political movement.
Thus, he necessarily finds himself in an insolvable dilemma.
What he *can* do contradicts all his previous actions, principles and immediate interests of his party, and what he
ought to do cannot be done. In a word, he is compelled to
represent not his party or his class, but the class for whose
domination the movement is then ripe. In the interests of
the movement he is compelled to advance the interests
of an alien class, and to feed his own class with phrases
and promises, and with the asseveration that the interests of that alien class are their own interests. Whoever

* [Italics by Plekhanov.]

is put into this awkward position is irrevocably lost."*

Hence it follows that Mr. Tikhomirov is greatly mistaken when he imagines that the seizure of power by the revolutionaries would be the "starting-point of the revolution." Quite the contrary: such a "seizure" would be a signal for reaction. It would not consolidate the influence of the country's progressive forces, but, having exhausted them in the first sterile effort, it would guarantee the triumph of the conservative and reactionary parties. Not only would the Russian revolution diverge from the example of the French revolution which our Jacobins treasure and which is the only comprehensible one for them, but in its development it would be the exact opposite of that revolution. Whereas up to a certain time every new wave of the French revolution brought on to the arena of history a more extreme party, our home-reared Jacobins would reduce to nil the corresponding period of the Russian revolution. Shattered and discredited, they would withdraw from the stage under a hail of hostile accusations and mockery, and the unorganized and disunited masses of the people, having no leaders, would be unable to overcome the systematic resistance of their enemies. At the very best the popular revolt would end in the overthrow of the remnants of the old regime without bringing the working people the reforms which most directly and immediately affect their interests.

As Marx notes, all facts of great importance in world history occur, as it were, twice: the first time as tragedy, the second as farce. The history of the French Jacobins is a majestic tragedy, full of burning interest. But the history of the conspiratorial plans of the modern Bakuninists (Russian and foreign) *despite the heroism* of individuals remains a farce whose tragicomicality lies in the complete inability of the cast to understand the meaning and character of the impending working-class revolution.

And so, "Russian socialism, as expressed in the Narodnaya Volya [People's Will] party," will be alien to the

* Quoted from Engels, *The Peasant War in Germany* (1850), a study of the revolt of 1524-1525. [Ed.]

great tasks of European socialism until it abandons for ever
its intermediary position between Bakunin's anarchism and
Tkachov's Blanquism,* i.e., until it acknowledges the bar-
renness of Mr. Tikhomirov's theoretical constructions.

But as these constructions are the last desperate attempt
to revive our revolutionary theories of the good old times,
our socialism, by raising itself to the height of such an ac-
knowledgment, will cease to be *"Russian"* and will merge
with world socialism "as expressed" in the works of Marx
and Engels and partly in those of Lassalle.

Its supporters will then understand that:

1. The *communist* revolution of the working class cannot
in any way grow out of the petty-bourgeois peasant socialism professed at present by nearly all our revolutionaries.

2. By the inherent character of its organization the rural
community tends first and foremost to give place to bourgeois, not communist, forms of social life.

3. In the transition to the latter its role will be not *active,*
but *passive;* it is not in a position to *advance* Russia on the
road to communism; it can only *offer less resistance* to that
advance than small individual landownership.

4. The initiative in the communist movement can be assumed only by the working class in our industrial centers,
the class,

5. Whose emancipation can be achieved only by its own
conscious efforts.

Once they have understood these simple truths, the Russian socialists "from the privileged sections" will put aside
all thoughts of seizing power, leaving that to our workers'
socialist party of the future. Then their efforts will be directed only *towards the creation of such a party and the
removal of all conditions which are unfavorable to its
growth and development. . . .*

The Social-Democrat, of course, will do only what he
can; but the advantage of his position is that *he can do
much more for the working class* than any other "socialist-

---

* The doctrine of the conspiratorial seizure of power proposed by the
Frenchman Auguste Blanqui, and repeated by the Russian Peter Tkachov.
[Ed.]

revolutionary." He will bring *consciousness* into the working class, and without that it is impossible to begin a serious struggle against capital. And once he brings that consciousness he will give the revolutionary movement a strength, endurance and intensity that cannot even be dreamed of when one remains on the old "programs."

And note that our Social-Democrat has no need at all to "fuss about (a typically Russian expression!) over the creation of the class in whose name he wishes to act." Only somebody who is completely ignorant of the economic relations in Russia today can be in the dark as to the indisputable fact that that class is partly already created and partly *being created* with increasing speed by the implacable course of social development. . . .

. . . We already know—and this we learn from the history of that same Western Europe—that only the first step was difficult for capitalism and that its uninterrupted advance from "West" to East is taking place with constantly increasing acceleration. Not only the development of capitalism in Russia cannot be as slow as it was in England, for example, its very existence cannot be so lasting as it has been fated to be in the "West European countries." Our capitalism will fade before it has time to blossom *completely*—a guarantee for which we find in the powerful influence of international relations. But neither is it possible to doubt that the course of affairs is advancing to its more or less complete victory. Neither unsubstantiated denials of an already existing fact nor grieved exclamations about the disintegration of the old "traditional" forms of the people's communal life—nothing will stop the advance of a country "which has entered the road of the natural law of its development." But this development will be more or less slow, the birth-pangs will be more or less painful, depending on the combination of all the social and international relations of the country in question. The more or less favorable character of that combination for the working class depends, in turn, on the conduct of those who have understood the meaning of the evolution which awaits their country.

LENIN: THE DOCTRINE OF THE PARTY

Vladimir Ilyich Lenin (born Ulyanov, 1869–1924) was one of the many Russian intellectuals who followed Plekhanov into Marxism. Lenin retained, however, a distinctive Russian stress on the role of tight organization, correctness of ideas, and dedicated leadership to achieve the hoped-for revolution. He expressed his central concept of the party in his pamphlet of 1902, What Is to Be Done?, a polemic against the "Economists" (as the Russian followers of Bernstein's revisionism were known). What Is to Be Done? contributed substantially to the split that took place among the Russian Marxists in 1903, when the Mensheviks rejected the dictatorial implications of Lenin's theory.

WHAT IS TO BE DONE?

We have said that our movement, much wider and deeper than the movement of the seventies, must be inspired with the same devoted determination and vigor that inspired the movement at that time. Indeed, no one, we think, has up to now doubted that the strength of the present-day movement lies in the awakening of the masses (principally, the industrial proletariat), and that its weakness lies in the lack of consciousness and initiative among the revolutionary leaders. . . .

In the previous chapter we pointed out how *universally* absorbed the educated youth of Russia was in the theories of Marxism in the middle of the nineties. The strikes that followed the famous St. Petersburg industrial war of 1896 assumed a similar wholesale character. The fact that these strikes spread over the whole of Russia clearly showed how deep the newly awakening popular movement was, and if we are to speak of the "spontaneous element" then, of course, it is this movement which, first and foremost, must be regarded as spontaneous. But there is spontaneity and spontaneity. Strikes occurred in Russia in the seventies and sixties (and even in the first half of the nineteenth

From V. I. Lenin, *What Is to Be Done?* (1902), in Lenin, *Selected Works* (Moscow, Foreign Languages Publishing House, 1950), Vol. I, Book 1, pp. 231-234, 242-245, 335-339.

century), and were accompanied by the "spontaneous" destruction of machinery, etc. Compared with these "riots" the strikes of the nineties might even be described as "conscious," to such an extent do they mark the progress which the working-class movement had made in that period. This shows that the "spontaneous element," in essence, represents nothing more nor less than consciousness in an *embryonic form*. Even the primitive riots expressed the awakening of consciousness to a certain extent: the workers were losing their agelong faith in the permanence of the system which oppressed them. They began . . . I shall not say to understand, but to sense the necessity for collective resistance, and definitely abandoned their slavish submission to their superiors. But this was, nevertheless, more in the nature of outbursts of desperation and vengeance than of *struggle*. The strikes of the nineties revealed far greater flashes of consciousness: definite demands were advanced, the strike was carefully timed, known cases and examples in other places were discussed, etc. While the riots were simply revolts of the oppressed, the systematic strikes represented the class struggle in embryo, but only in embryo. Taken by themselves, these strikes were simply trade union struggles, but not yet Social-Democratic struggles. They testified to the awakening antagonisms between workers and employers, but the workers were not, and could not be, conscious of the irreconcilable antagonism of their interests to the whole of the modern political and social system, i.e., theirs was not yet Social-Democratic consciousness. In this sense, the strikes of the nineties, in spite of the enormous progress they represented as compared with the "riots," remained a purely spontaneous movement.

We have said that *there could not yet be* Social-Democratic consciousness among the workers. It could only be brought to them from without. The history of all countries shows that the working class, exclusively by its own effort, is able to develop only trade union consciousness, i.e., the conviction that it is necessary to combine in unions, fight the employers and strive to compel the government to pass necessary labor legislation, etc. The theory of Socialism,

however, grew out of the philosophic, historical and economic theories that were elaborated by the educated
representatives of the propertied classes, the intellectuals.
According to their social status, the founders of modern
scientific Socialism, Marx and Engels, themselves belonged
to the bourgeois intelligentsia. In the very same way, in
Russia, the theoretical doctrine of Social-Democracy arose
quite independently of the spontaneous growth of the
working-class movement, it arose as a natural and inevitable
outcome of the development of ideas among the revolutionary socialist intelligentsia. At the time of which we are
speaking, i.e., the middle of the nineties, this doctrine not
only represented the completely formulated program of the
Emancipation of Labor group,* but had already won over
to its side the majority of the revolutionary youth in Russia.

Hence, we had both the spontaneous awakening of the
masses of the workers, the awakening to conscious life and
conscious struggle, and a revolutionary youth, armed with
the Social-Democratic theory, eager to come into contact
with the workers. In this connection it is particularly important to state the oft-forgotten (and comparatively little-
known) fact that the *early* Social-Democrats of that period
zealously carried on economic agitation (being guided in
this by the really useful instructions contained in the pamphlet *On Agitation* that was still in manuscript), but they
did not regard this as their sole task. On the contrary, *right
from the very beginning* they advanced the widest historical tasks of Russian Social-Democracy in general, and
the task of overthrowing the autocracy in particular. . . .

. . . The adherents of the "pure" working-class movement,
the worshippers of the closest "organic" (the term used by
the *Rabocheye Dyelo*†) contacts with the proletarian struggle, the opponents of any nonworker intelligentsia (even if
it be a socialist intelligentsia) are compelled, in order to
defend their positions, to resort to the arguments of the
bourgeois "pure" trade unionists. This shows that from the

* The Marxist organization in St. Petersburg in the 1890's. [Ed.]
† "The Workers' Cause," magazine of the "Economists." [Ed.]

very outset the *Rabochaya Mysl** began—unconsciously—to carry out the program of the *Credo*.† This shows (something the *Rabocheye Dyelo* cannot understand at all) that *all* worship of the spontaneity of the working-class movement, all belittling of the role of "the conscious element," of the role of Social-Democracy, *means, quite irrespective of whether the belittler wants to or not, strengthening the influence of the bourgeois ideology over the workers.* All those who talk about "overrating the importance of ideology," about exaggerating the role of the conscious element, etc., imagine that the pure working-class movement can work out, and will work out, an independent ideology for itself, if only the workers "wrest their fate from the hands of the leaders." . . .

Since there can be no talk of an independent ideology being developed by the masses of the workers themselves in the process of their movement‡ the *only* choice is: either the bourgeois or the socialist ideology. There is no middle course (for humanity has not created a "third" ideology, and, moreover, in a society torn by class antagonisms there can never be a non-class or above-class ideology). Hence, to belittle the socialist ideology *in any way,* to *turn away from it in the slightest degree* means to strengthen bourgeois ideology. There is a lot of talk about spontaneity, but the *spontaneous* development of the working-class movement leads to its becoming subordinated to the bourgeois ideology, *leads to its developing according to the program*

---

* "The Workers' Idea," a St. Petersburg labor newspaper. [Ed.]

† A program of the "Economists." [Ed.]

‡ This does not mean, of course, that the workers have no part in creating such an ideology. But they take part not as workers, but as socialist theoreticians, as Proudhons and Weitlings; in other words, they take part only when, and to the extent that they are able, more or less, to acquire the knowledge of their age and advance that knowledge. And in order that workingmen *may be able to do this more often,* every effort must be made to raise the level of the consciousness of the workers generally; the workers must not confine themselves to the artificially restricted limits of *"literature for workers"* but should learn to master *general literature* to an increasing degree. It would be even more true to say "are not confined," instead of "must not confine themselves," because the workers themselves wish to read and do read all that is written for the intelligentsia and it is only a few (bad) intellectuals who believe that it is sufficient "for the workers" to be told a few things about factory conditions, and to have repeated to them over and over again what has long been known. [Lenin's note.]

of the *Credo,* for the spontaneous working-class movement
is trade unionism . . . , and trade unionism means the ideological enslavement of the workers by the bourgeoisie.
Hence, our task, the task of Social-Democracy, is to *combat spontaneity,* to *divert* the working-class movement from
this spontaneous, trade-unionist striving to come under the
wing of the bourgeoisie, and to bring it under the wing of
revolutionary Social-Democracy. The phrase employed by
the authors of the "economic" letter in the *Iskra,** No. 12,
about the efforts of the most inspired ideologists not being
able to divert the working-class movement from the path
that is determined by the interaction of the material elements and the material environment, *is absolutely tantamount* therefore *to the abandonment of Socialism,* and if
only the authors of this letter were capable of fearlessly,
consistently and thoroughly considering what they say, as
everyone who enters the arena of literary and public activity should do, there would be nothing left for them but
to "fold their useless arms over their empty breasts" and
. . . leave the field of action to Messrs. the Struves and
Prokopoviches who are dragging the working-class movement "along the line of least resistance," i.e., along the line
of bourgeois trade unionism, or to the Zubatovs, who are
dragging it along the line of clerical and gendarme "ideology."† . . .

I assert that it is far more difficult to wipe out a dozen
wise men than a hundred fools. And this position I shall
defend no matter how much you instigate the crowd
against me for my "antidemocratic" views, etc. As I have
already said time and again that by "wise men," in connection with organization, I mean *professional revolutionaries,* irrespective of whether they are trained from among
students or workingmen. I assert: 1) that no revolutionary
movement can endure without a stable organization of
leaders that maintains continuity; 2) that the wider the

* "The Spark," a Marxist newspaper.
† P. B. Struve—a former Marxist who shifted to liberalism; S. N. Proko-
povich—a spokesman of the "Economists"; S. V. Zubatov—an official
who tried to promote trade unions controlled by the police. [Ed.]

masses spontaneously drawn into the struggle, forming
the basis of the movement and participating in it, the more
urgent the need of such an organization, and the more
solid this organization must be (for it is much easier for
demagogues to sidetrack the more backward sections of
the masses); 3) that such an organization must consist
chiefly of people professionally engaged in revolutionary
activity; 4) that in an autocratic state, the more we *confine*
the membership of such an organization to people who are
professionally engaged in revolutionary activity and who
have been professionally trained in the art of combating
the political police, the more difficult will it be to wipe
out such an organization, and 5) the *greater* will be the
number of people of the working class and of the other
classes of society who will be able to join the movement
and perform active work in it.

I invite our Economists, terrorists and "Economists-
terrorists" to confute these propositions. At the moment,
I shall deal only with the last two points. The question as
to whether it is easier to wipe out "a dozen wise men" or
"a hundred fools" reduces itself to the question we have
considered above, namely, whether it is possible to have
a mass *organization* when the maintenance of strict secrecy
is essential. We can never give a mass organization that
degree of secrecy without which there can be no question
of persistent and continuous struggle against the government. But to concentrate all secret functions in the hands
of as small a number of professional revolutionaries as
possible does not mean that the latter will "do the thinking for all" and that the crowd will not take an active part
in the *movement*. On the contrary, the crowd will advance
from its ranks increasing numbers of professional revolutionaries; for it will know that it is not enough for a few
students and for a few workingmen waging the economic
struggle, to gather together and form a "committee," but
that it takes years to train oneself to be a professional
revolutionary; the crowd will "think" not of amateurish
methods alone but of such training. The centralization of
the secret functions of the *organization* by no means im-

plies the centralization of all the functions of the *movement*. The active participation of the widest mass in the illegal press will not diminish because a "dozen" professional revolutionaries centralize the secret functions connected with this work; on the contrary, it will *increase* tenfold. In this way, and in this way alone, will we ensure that reading of illegal literature, writing for it, and to some extent even distributing it, will *almost cease to be secret work*, for the police will soon come to realize the folly and futility of setting the whole judicial and administrative machine into motion to intercept every copy of a publication that is being broadcast in thousands. This applies not only to the press, but to every function of the movement, even to demonstrations. The active and widespread participation of the masses will not suffer; on the contrary, it will benefit by the fact that a "dozen" experienced revolutionaries, trained professionally no less than the police, will centralize all the secret aspects of the work—drawing up leaflets, working out approximate plans and appointing bodies of leaders for each urban district, for each factory district and for each educational institution, etc. (I know that exception will be taken to my "undemocratic" views, but I shall reply fully to this anything but intelligent objection later on.) The centralization of the most secret functions in an organization of revolutionaries will not diminish, but rather increase the extent and quality of the activity of a large number of other organizations which are intended for a broad public and are therefore as loose and as non-secret as possible, such as workers' trade unions, workers' self-education circles and circles for reading illegal literature, socialist and also democratic circles among *all* other sections of the population, etc., etc. We must have such circles, trade unions and organizations everywhere in *as large a number as possible* and with the widest variety of functions; but it would be absurd and dangerous to *confuse* them with the organization of *revolutionaries*, to obliterate the border line between them, to dim still more the masses' already incredibly hazy appreciation of the fact that in order to "serve" the mass movement we must have people who will devote themselves exclusively to Social-Democratic activities, and that such people must *train* themselves patiently and steadfastly to be professional revolutionaries.

Yes, this appreciation has become incredibly dim. Our chief sin with regard to organization is that *by our amateurishness we have lowered the prestige of revolutionaries in Russia.* A person who is flabby and shaky in questions of theory, who has a narrow outlook, who pleads the spontaneity of the masses as an excuse for his own sluggishness, who resembles a trade union secretary more than a people's tribune, who is unable to conceive of a broad and bold plan that would command the respect even of opponents, and who is inexperienced and clumsy in his own professional art—the art of combating the political police —why, such a man is not a revolutionary but a wretched amateur!

Let no active worker take offense at these frank remarks, for as far as insufficient training is concerned, I apply them first and foremost to myself. I used to work in a circle that set itself very wide, all-embracing tasks; and all of us, members of that circle, suffered painfully, acutely from the realization that we were proving ourselves to be amateurs at a moment in history when we might have been able to say, paraphrasing a well-known epigram: "Give us an organization of revolutionaries, and we shall overturn Russia!" And the more I recall the burning sense of shame I then experienced, the more bitter are my feelings towards those pseudo Social-Democrats whose teachings "bring disgrace on the calling of a revolutionary," who fail to understand that our task is not to champion the degrading of the revolutionary to the level of an amateur, but to *raise* the amateurs to the level of revolutionaries.

LENIN: THE THEORY OF WORLD CAPITALISM

At the turn of the century, a number of European Marxists published books in which they attempted to give an economic explanation of imperialism and colonial expansion. During World War I, while he was still an exile in Switzerland, Lenin wrote Imperialism—The Highest Stage of Capitalism, *to argue that capitalism led inevitably to imperialism and war. Since the Russian Revolution, this book has been the foundation for Communist thinking about international relations.*

IMPERIALISM—THE HIGHEST STAGE OF CAPITALISM

We have seen that in its economic essence imperialism is monopoly capitalism. This in itself determines its place in history, for monopoly that grows out of the soil of free competition, and precisely out of free competition, is the transition from the capitalist system to a higher social-economic order. We must take special note of the four principal types of monopoly, or principal manifestations of monopoly capitalism, which are characteristic of the epoch we are examining.

Firstly, monopoly arose out of a very high stage of development of the concentration of production. This refers to the monopolist capitalist combines, cartels, syndicates and trusts. We have seen the important part these play in present-day economic life. At the beginning of the twentieth century, monopolies had acquired complete supremacy in the advanced countries, and although the first steps towards the formation of the cartels were first taken by countries enjoying the protection of high tariffs (Germany, America), Great Britain, with her system of free trade, revealed the same basic phenomenon, only a little later, namely, the birth of monopoly out of the concentration of production.

Secondly, monopolies have stimulated the seizure of the

From V. I. Lenin, *Imperialism—The Highest Stage of Capitalism* (1916), in Lenin, *Selected Works* (Moscow, Foreign Languages Publishing House, 1950), Vol. I, Book 2, pp. 562-564, 566-567.

most important sources of raw materials, especially for the basic and most highly cartelized industries in capitalist society: the coal and iron industries. The monopoly of the most important sources of raw materials has enormously increased the power of big capital, and has sharpened the antagonism between cartelized and noncartelized industry.

Thirdly, monopoly has sprung from the banks. The banks have developed from humble middlemen enterprises into the monopolists of finance capital. Some three to five of the biggest banks in each of the foremost capitalist countries have achieved the "personal union" of industrial and bank capital, and have concentrated in their hands the control of thousands upon thousands of millions which form the greater part of the capital and income of entire countries. A financial oligarchy, which throws a close network of dependence relationships over all the economic and political institutions of present-day bourgeois society without exception—such is the most striking manifestation of this monopoly.

Fourthly, monopoly has grown out of colonial policy. To the numerous "old" motives of colonial policy, finance capital has added the struggle for the sources of raw materials, for the export of capital, for "spheres of influence," i.e., for spheres for profitable deals, concessions, monopolist profits and so on, and finally, for economic territory in general. When the colonies of the European powers in Africa, for instance, comprised only one tenth of that territory (as was the case in 1876), colonial policy was able to develop by methods other than those of monopoly—by the "free grabbing" of territories, so to speak. But when nine tenths of Africa had been seized (by 1900), when the whole world had been divided up, there was inevitably ushered in the era of monopoly ownership of colonies and, consequently, of particularly intense struggle for the division and the redivision of the world.

The extent to which monopolist capital has intensified all the contradictions of capitalism is generally known. It is sufficient to mention the high cost of living and the tyranny of the cartels. This intensification of contradictions constitutes the most powerful driving force of the transitional period of history, which began from the time of the final victory of world finance capital.

Monopolies, oligarchy, the striving for domination instead of striving for liberty, the exploitation of an increasing number of small or weak nations by a handful of the richest or most powerful nations—all these have given birth to those distinctive characteristics of imperialism which compel us to define it as parasitic or decaying capitalism. More and more prominently there emerges, as one of the tendencies of imperialism, the creation of the "rentier state," the usurer state, in which the bourgeoisie to an ever increasing degree lives on the proceeds of capital exports and by "clipping coupons." It would be a mistake to believe that this tendency to decay precludes the rapid growth of capitalism. It does not. In the epoch of imperialism, certain branches of industry, certain strata of the bourgeoisie and certain countries betray, to a greater or lesser degree, now one and now another of these tendencies. On the whole, capitalism is growing far more rapidly than before; but this growth is not only becoming more and more uneven in general, its unevenness also manifests itself, in particular, in the decay of the countries which are richest in capital (England). . . .

From all that has been said in this book on the economic essence of imperialism, it follows that we must define it as capitalism in transition, or, more precisely, as moribund capitalism. It is very instructive in this respect to note that the bourgeois economists, in describing modern capitalism, frequently employ catchwords and phrases like "interlocking," "absence of isolation," etc.; "in conformity with their functions and course of development," banks are "not purely private business enterprises; they are more and more outgrowing the sphere of purely private business regulation." And this very Riesser,* who uttered the words just quoted, declares with all seriousness that the "proph-

* A German economist. [Ed.]

ecy" of the Marxists concerning "socialization" has "not come true"!

What then does this catchword "interlocking" express? It merely expresses the most striking feature of the process going on before our eyes. It shows that the observer counts the separate trees, but cannot see the wood. It slavishly copies the superficial, the fortuitous, the chaotic. It reveals the observer as one who is overwhelmed by the mass of raw material and is utterly incapable of appreciating its meaning and importance. Ownership of shares, the relations between owners of private property "interlock in a haphazard way." But underlying this interlocking, its very base, is the changing social relations of production. When a big enterprise assumes gigantic proportions, and, on the basis of an exact computation of mass data, organizes according to plan the supply of primary raw materials to the extent of two thirds, or three fourths of all that is necessary for tens of millions of people; when the raw materials are transported in a systematic and organized manner to the most suitable place of production, sometimes hundreds or thousands of miles; when a single center directs all the consecutive stages of work right up to the manufacture of numerous varieties of finished articles; when these products are distributed according to a single plan among tens and hundreds of millions of consumers (the distribution of oil in America and Germany by the American "oil trust")—then it becomes evident that we have socialization of production, and not mere "interlocking"; that private economic and private property relations constitute a shell which no longer fits its contents, a shell which must inevitably decay if its removal by artificial means be delayed; a shell which may continue in a state of decay for a fairly long period (if, at the worst, the cure of the opportunist abscess is protracted), but which will inevitably be removed.

LENIN: THE DICTATORSHIP OF THE PROLETARIAT

Between the February and October Revolutions of 1917, while Lenin was in hiding, waiting for the opportunity to lead his party to victory, he wrote an extensive treatise on the Marxian theory of the state and its application to the Russian Revolution. This work, The State and Revolution, *is commonly accepted by both Communists and non-Communists as the foundation of the Communist theory of government, although its stress on rule by the working class and the "withering away of the state" was soon outdated by the evolution of Communism into totalitarianism.*

THE STATE AND REVOLUTION

I. CLASS SOCIETY AND THE STATE

The State as the Product of the Irreconcilability of Class Antagonisms

What is now happening to Marx's teaching has, in the course of history, happened repeatedly to the teachings of revolutionary thinkers and leaders of oppressed classes struggling for emancipation. During the lifetime of great revolutionaries, the oppressing classes constantly hounded them, received their teachings with the most savage malice, the most furious hatred and the most unscrupulous campaigns of lies and slander. After their death, attempts are made to convert them into harmless icons, to canonize them, so to say, and to surround their *names* with a certain halo for the "consolation" of the oppressed classes and with the object of duping the latter, while at the same time emasculating the *essence* of the revolutionary teaching, blunting its revolutionary edge and vulgarizing it. At the present time, the bourgeoisie and the opportunists within the working-class movement concur in this "doctoring" of Marxism. They omit, obliterate and distort the revolutionary side of this teaching, its revolutionary soul. They push

From V. I. Lenin, *The State and Revolution* (1917), in Lenin, *Selected Works* (Moscow, Foreign Languages Publishing House, 1950), Vol. II, Book 1, pp. 202-204, 213-216, 242-244, 249-251, 289-294, 299-300.

to the foreground and extol what is or seems acceptable
to the bourgeoisie. All the social-chauvinists* are now
"Marxists" (don't laugh!). And more and more frequently,
German bourgeois scholars, but yesterday specialists in the
annihilation of Marxism, are speaking of the "national-
German" Marx, who, they aver, educated the workers'
unions which are so splendidly organized for the purpose
of conducting a predatory war!

In such circumstances, in view of the unprecedentedly
widespread distortion of Marxism, our prime task is to *re-
establish* what Marx really taught on the subject of the
state. . . .

Let us begin with the most popular of Engels' works,
*The Origin of the Family, Private Property and the
State.* . . .

Summing up his historical analysis, Engels says:

"The state is, therefore, by no means a power forced
on society from without; just as little is it 'the reality of
the ethical idea,' 'the image and reality of reason,' as Hegel
maintains. Rather, it is a product of society at a certain
stage of development; it is the admission that this society
has become entangled in an insoluble contradiction with
itself, that it is cleft into irreconcilable antagonisms which
it is powerless to dispel. But in order that these antagonisms, classes with conflicting economic interests, might
not consume themselves and society in sterile struggle, a
power seemingly standing above society became necessary
for the purpose of moderating the conflict, of keeping it
within the bounds of 'order'; and this power, arisen out of
society, but placing itself above it, and increasingly alienat-
ing itself from it, is the state."

This expresses with perfect clarity the basic idea of
Marxism on the question of the historical role and the
meaning of the state. The state is the product and the
manifestation of the *irreconcilability* of class antagonisms.
The state arises when, where and to the extent that class

* A reference to the Social Democrats who supported their national war
effort on either side in World War I. [Ed.]

antagonisms objectively *cannot* be reconciled. And, conversely, the existence of the state proves that the class antagonisms are irreconcilable. . . .

The "Withering Away" of the State
and Violent Revolution

Engels' words regarding the "withering away" of the state are so widely known, they are so often quoted, and so clearly reveal the essence of the customary adulteration of Marxism to look like opportunism that we must deal with them in detail. We shall quote the whole argument from which they are taken.

"The proletariat seizes the state power and transforms the means of production in the first instance into state property. But in doing this, it puts an end to itself as proletariat, it puts an end to all class differences and class antagonisms; it puts an end also to the state as state. Former society, moving in class antagonisms, had need of the state, that is, an organization of the exploiting class at each period for the maintenance of its external conditions of production; that is, therefore, mainly for the forcible holding down of the exploited class in the conditions of oppression (slavery, villeinage or serfdom, wage labor) determined by the existing mode of production. The state was the official representative of society as a whole, its summation in a visible corporation; but it was this only in so far as it was the state of that class which itself, in its epoch, represented society as a whole: in ancient times, the state of the slaveowning citizens; in the Middle Ages, of the feudal nobility; in our epoch, of the bourgeoisie. When ultimately it becomes really representative of society as a whole, it makes itself superfluous. As soon as there is no longer any class of society to be held in subjection; as soon as, along with class domination and the struggle for individual existence based on the anarchy of production hitherto, the collisions and excesses arising from these have also been abolished, there is nothing more to be repressed which would make a special repressive force, a state, necessary. The first act in which the state really comes forward as the representative of society as a whole —the taking possession of the means of production in the name of society—is at the same time its last independent act as a state. The interference of the state power in social relations becomes superfluous in one sphere after another, and then ceases of itself. The government of persons is replaced by the administration of things and the direction of the processes of production. The state is not 'abolished,' *it withers away*. It is from this standpoint that we must appraise the phrase 'free people's state'—both its temporary justification for agitational purposes, and its ultimate scientific inadequacy—and also the demand of the so-called anarchists that the state should be abolished overnight." (*Herr Eugen Dühring's Revolution in Science [Anti-Dühring].*)

It may be said without fear of error that of this argument of Engels' which is so remarkably rich in ideas, only one point has become an integral part of socialist thought among modern socialist parties, namely, that according to Marx the state "withers away"—as distinct from the anarchist doctrine of the "abolition" of the state. To prune Marxism in such a manner is to reduce it to opportunism, for such an "interpretation" only leaves a vague notion of a slow, even, gradual change, of absence of leaps and storms, of absence of revolution. The current, widespread, mass, if one may say so, conception of the "withering away" of the state undoubtedly means toning down, if not repudiating, revolution.

Such an "interpretation," however, is the crudest distortion of Marxism, advantageous only to the bourgeoisie; in point of theory, it is based on a disregard for the most important circumstances and considerations indicated, say, in Engels' "summary" argument we have just quoted in full.

In the first place, at the very outset of his argument Engels says that, in seizing state power, the proletariat thereby "abolishes the state as state." It is not "good form" to ponder over the meaning of this. Generally, it is either

ignored altogether, or is considered to be something in the
nature of "Hegelian weakness" on Engels' part. As a matter of fact, however, these words briefly express the experience of one of the greatest proletarian revolutions, the
Paris Commune of 1871, of which we shall speak in greater
detail in its proper place. As a matter of fact, Engels speaks
here of the proletarian revolution "abolishing" the *bourgeois* state, while the words about the state withering away
refer to the remnants of the *proletarian* state *after* the
socialist revolution. According to Engels the bourgeois
state does not "wither away," but is "*a b o l i s h e d*" by
the proletariat in the course of the revolution. What withers away after this revolution is the proletarian state or
semistate.

Secondly, the state is a "special repressive force." Engels
gives this splendid and extremely profound definition here
with the utmost lucidity. And from it follows that the
"special repressive force" for the suppression of the proletariat by the bourgeoisie, of millions of toilers by hand-
fuls of the rich, must be replaced by a "special repressive
force" for the suppression of the bourgeoisie by the proletariat (the dictatorship of the proletariat). This is precisely
what is meant by "abolition of the state as state." This is
precisely the "act" of taking possession of the means of
production in the name of society. And it is self-evident
that *such* a replacement of one (bourgeois) "special force"
by another (proletarian) "special force" cannot possibly
take place in the form of "withering away."

Thirdly, in speaking of the state "withering away," and
the even more graphic and colorful "ceasing of itself,"
Engels refers quite clearly and definitely to the period
a f t e r "the state has taken possession of the means of
production in the name of the whole of society," that is,
a f t e r the socialist revolution. We all know that the political form of the "state" at that time is the most complete
democracy. But it never enters the head of any of the opportunists who shamelessly distort Marxism that Engels
is consequently speaking here of *d e m o c r a c y* "ceasing
of itself," or "withering away." This seems very strange at

first sight; but it is "incomprehensible" only to those who have not pondered over the fact that democracy is *a l s o* a state and that, consequently, democracy will also disappear when the state disappears. Revolution alone can "abolish" the bourgeois state. The state in general, i.e., the most complete democracy, can only "wither away.". . .

III. THE STATE AND REVOLUTION. EXPERIENCE OF THE PARIS COMMUNE OF 1871. MARX'S ANALYSIS . . .

With What Is the Smashed State Machine
to Be Replaced? . . .

. . . The Commune appears to have replaced the smashed state machine "only" by fuller democracy: abolition of the standing army; all officials to be elected and subject to recall. But as a matter of fact this "only" signifies a gigantic replacement of certain institutions by other institutions of a fundamentally different order. This is exactly a case of "quantity becoming transformed into quality": democracy, introduced as fully and consistently as is at all conceivable, is transformed from bourgeois democracy into proletarian democracy; from the state (=a special force for the suppression of a particular class) into something which is no longer really the state.

It is still necessary to suppress the bourgeoisie and crush its resistance. This was particularly necessary for the Commune; and one of the reasons for its defeat was that it did not do this with sufficient determination. But the organ of suppression is now the majority of the population, and not a minority, as was always the case under slavery, serfdom and wage slavery. And since the majority of the people *itself* suppresses its oppressors, a "special force" for suppression is *n o l o n g e r n e c e s s a r y!* In this sense the state *begins to wither away.* Instead of the special institutions of a privileged minority (privileged officialdom, the chiefs of the standing army), the majority itself can directly fulfil all these functions, and the more the functions of state power devolve upon the people as a whole the less need is there for the existence of this power.

In this connection the following measures of the Commune emphasized by Marx are particularly noteworthy: the abolition of all representation allowances, and of all monetary privileges in the case of officials, the reduction of the remuneration of *all* servants of the state to the level of *"workmen's wages."* This shows more clearly than anything else the *turn* from bourgeois democracy to proletarian democracy, from the democracy of the oppressors to the democracy of the oppressed classes, from the state as a *"special force"* for the suppression of a particular class to the suppression of the oppressors by the *general force* of the majority of the people—the workers and the peasants. And it is precisely on this particularly striking point, perhaps the most important as far as the problem of the state is concerned, that the teachings of Marx have been most completely forgotten! In popular commentaries, the number of which is legion, this is not mentioned. It is "good form" to keep silent about it as if it were a piece of old-fashioned "naïveté," just as the Christians, after their religion had been given the status of a state religion, "forgot" the "naïveté" of primitive Christianity with its democratic revolutionary spirit.

The reduction of the remuneration of the highest state officials seems to be "simply" a demand of naive, primitive democracy. One of the "founders" of modern opportunism, the ex-Social-Democrat, Eduard Bernstein, has more than once indulged in repeating the vulgar bourgeois jeers at "primitive" democracy. Like all opportunists, and like the present Kautskyites,* he utterly failed to understand that, first of all, the transition from capitalism to Socialism is *impossible* without a certain "reversion" to "primitive" democracy (for how else can the majority, and then the whole population without exception, proceed to discharge state functions?); and, secondly, that "primitive democracy" based on capitalism and capitalist culture is not the same as primitive democracy in prehistoric or precapitalist times. Capitalist culture has *created* large-scale production,

* Followers of the "orthodox" Marxist Karl Kautsky, who were democratic but doctrinaire. [Ed.]

factories, railways, the postal service, telephones, etc., and *on this basis* the great majority of the functions of the old "state power" have become so simplified and can be reduced to such exceedingly simple operations of registration, filing and checking that they can be easily performed by every literate person, can quite easily be performed for ordinary "workmen's wages," and that these functions can (and must) be stripped of every shadow of privilege, of every semblance of "official grandeur."

All officials, without exception, elected and subject to recall *at any time*, their salaries reduced to the level of ordinary, "workmen's wages"—these simple and "self-evident" democratic measures, while completely uniting the interests of the workers and the majority of the peasants, at the same time serve as a bridge leading from capitalism to Socialism. These measures concern the reconstruction of the state, the purely political reconstruction of society; but, of course, they acquire their full meaning and significance only in connection with the "expropriation of the expropriators" either being accomplished or in preparation, i.e., with the transformation of capitalist private ownership of the means of production into social ownership. . . .

Abolition of Parliamentarism . . .

There can be no thought of abolishing the bureaucracy at once, everywhere and completely. That is utopia. But to *smash* the old bureaucratic machine at once and to begin immediately to construct a new one that will permit to abolish gradually all bureaucracy—this is *n o t* utopia, this is the experience of the Commune, this is the direct and immediate task of the revolutionary proletariat.

Capitalism simplifies the functions of "state" administration; it makes it possible to cast "bossing" aside and to confine the whole matter to the organization of the proletarians (as the ruling class), which will hire "workers, foremen and bookkeepers" in the name of the whole of society.

We are not utopians, we do not indulge in "dreams" of dispensing *at once* with all administration, with all sub-

ordination; these anarchist dreams, based upon a lack of
understanding of the tasks of the proletarian dictatorship,
are totally alien to Marxism, and, as a matter of fact, serve
only to postpone the socialist revolution until people are
different. No, we want the socialist revolution with people
as they are now, with people who cannot dispense with
subordination, control and "foremen and bookkeepers."

But the subordination must be to the armed vanguard
of all the exploited and toiling people, i.e., to the proletariat. A beginning can and must be made at once, overnight,
of replacing the specific "bossing" of state officials by the
simple functions of "foremen and bookkeepers," functions
which are already fully within the capacity of the average
city dweller and can well be performed for "workmen's
wages."

We ourselves, the workers, will organize large-scale production on the basis of what capitalism has already created,
relying on our own experience as workers, establishing
strict, iron discipline supported by the state power of the
armed workers; we will reduce the role of the state officials
to that of simply carrying out our instructions as responsible, revocable, modestly paid "foremen and bookkeepers"
(of course, with the aid of technicians of all sorts, types
and degrees). This is *our* proletarian task, this is what we
can and must *start* with in accomplishing the proletarian
revolution. Such a beginning, on the basis of large-scale
production, will of itself lead to the gradual "withering
away" of all bureaucracy, to the gradual creation of an
order, an order without quotation marks, an order bearing
no similarity to wage slavery, an order in which the functions of control and accounting—becoming more and more
simple—will be performed by each in turn, will then become a habit and will finally die out as the *special* functions of a special section of the population.

A witty German Social-Democrat of the seventies of
the last century called the *postal service* an example of the
socialist economic system. This is very true. At present the
postal service is a business organized on the lines of a
state-*capitalist* monopoly. Imperialism is gradually trans-

forming all trusts into organizations of a similar type, in which, standing over the "common" toilers, who are over-worked and starved, is the same bourgeois bureaucracy. But the mechanism of social management is here already to hand. We have but to overthrow the capitalists, to crush the resistance of these exploiters with the iron hand of the armed workers, to smash the bureaucratic machine of the modern state—and we shall have a splendidly-equipped mechanism, freed from the "parasite," a mechanism which can very well be set going by the united workers them-selves, who will hire technicians, foremen and bookkeepers, and pay them *all*, as, indeed, *all* "state" officials in general, a workman's wage. Here is a concrete, practical task, im-mediately possible of fulfilment in relation to all trusts, a task that will rid the toilers of exploitation and take account of what the Commune had already begun to practice (par-ticularly in building up the state).

To organize the *whole* national economy on the lines of the postal service, so that the technicians, foremen, bookkeepers, as well as *all* officials, shall receive salaries no higher than "a workman's wage," all under the control and leadership of the armed proletariat—this is our imme-diate aim. It is such a state, standing on such an economic foundation, that we need. This is what will bring about the abolition of parliamentarism and the preservation of repre-sentative institutions. This is what will rid the laboring classes of the prostitution of these institutions by the bour-geoisie. . . .

V. THE ECONOMIC BASIS OF THE WITHERING AWAY OF THE STATE . . .

The Transition from Capitalism to Communism . . .

In capitalist society, providing it develops under the most favorable conditions, we have a more or less complete de-mocracy in the democratic republic. But this democracy is always hemmed in by the narrow limits set by capitalist exploitation, and consequently always remains, in reality, a democracy for the minority, only for the propertied classes, only for the rich. Freedom in capitalist society always remains about the same as it was in the ancient Greek republics: freedom for the slaveowners. Owing to the conditions of capitalist exploitation the modern wage slaves are so crushed by want and poverty that "they cannot be bothered with democracy," "they cannot be bothered with politics"; in the ordinary peaceful course of events the majority of the population is debarred from participation in public and political life.

The correctness of this statement is perhaps most clearly confirmed by Germany, precisely because in that country constitutional legality steadily endured for a remarkably long time—for nearly half a century (1871–1914)—and during this period Social-Democracy there was able to achieve far more than in other countries in the way of "utilizing legality," and organized a larger proportion of the workers into a political party than anywhere else in the world.

What is this largest proportion of politically conscious and active wage slaves that has so far been observed in capitalist society? One million members of the Social-Democratic Party—out of fifteen million wageworkers! Three million organized in trade unions—out of fifteen million!

Democracy for an insignificant minority, democracy for the rich—that is the democracy of capitalist society. If we look more closely into the machinery of capitalist democracy, we shall see everywhere, in the "petty"—supposedly petty—details of the suffrage (residential qualification, exclusion of women, etc.), in the technique of the representative institutions, in the actual obstacles to the right of assembly (public buildings are not for "beggars"!), in the purely capitalist organization of the daily press, etc., etc.—we shall see restriction after restriction upon democracy. These restrictions, exceptions, exclusions, obstacles for the poor, seem slight, especially in the eyes of one who has never known want himself and has never been in close contact with the oppressed classes in their mass life (and nine tenths, if not ninety-nine hundredths, of the bourgeois publicists and politicians are of this category); but in their sum total these restrictions exclude and squeeze out the poor from politics, from active participation in democracy.

Marx grasped this *e s s e n c e* of capitalist democracy splendidly, when, in analyzing the experience of the Commune, he said that the oppressed are allowed once every few years to decide which particular representatives of the oppressing class shall represent and repress them in parliament!

But from this capitalist democracy—that is inevitably narrow, and stealthily pushes aside the poor, and is therefore hypocritical and false to the core—forward development does not proceed simply, directly and smoothly towards "greater and greater democracy," as the liberal professors and petty bourgeois opportunists would have us believe. No, forward development, i.e., towards Communism, proceeds through the dictatorship of the proletariat, and cannot do otherwise, for the *resistance* of the capitalist exploiters cannot be *broken* by anyone else or in any other way.

And the dictatorship of the proletariat, i.e., the organization of the vanguard of the oppressed as the ruling class for the purpose of suppressing the oppressors, cannot result merely in an expansion of democracy. *Simultaneously* with an immense expansion of democracy, which *f o r   t h e   f i r s t   t i m e* becomes democracy for the poor, democracy for the people, and not democracy for the moneybags, the dictatorship of the proletariat imposes a series of restrictions on the freedom of the oppressors, the exploiters, the capitalists. We must suppress them in order to free humanity from wage slavery, their resistance must be crushed by force; it is clear that where there is suppression, where there is violence, there is no freedom and no democracy.

Engels expressed this splendidly in his letter to Bebel when he said, as the reader will remember, that "the proletariat uses the state not in the interests of freedom but in order to hold down its adversaries, and as soon as it becomes possible to speak of freedom the state as such ceases to exist."

Democracy for the vast majority of the people, and suppression by force, i.e., exclusion from democracy, of the exploiters and oppressors of the people—this is the change democracy undergoes during the *transition* from capitalism to Communism.

Only in communist society, when the resistance of the capitalists has been completely crushed, when the capitalists have disappeared, when there are no classes (i.e., when there is no difference between the members of society as regards their relation to the social means of production), *only* then "the state . . . ceases to exist," and it *"becomes possible to speak of freedom."* Only then will there become possible and be realized a truly complete democracy, democracy without any exceptions whatever. And only then will democracy begin to *wither away,* owing to the simple fact that, freed from capitalist slavery, from the untold horrors, savagery, absurdities and infamies of capitalist exploitation, people will gradually *b e c o m e   a c c u s - t o m e d* to observing the elementary rules of social intercourse that have been known for centuries and repeated for thousands of years in all copybook maxims; they will become accustomed to observing them without force, without compulsion, without subordination, *w i t h o u t   t h e s p e c i a l   a p p a r a t u s* for compulsion which is called the state.

The expression "the state *withers away*" is very well chosen, for it indicates both the gradual and the spontaneous nature of the process. Only habit can, and undoubtedly will, have such an effect; for we see around us on millions of occasions how readily people become accustomed to observing the necessary rules of social intercourse when there is no exploitation, when there is nothing that rouses indignation, nothing that evokes protest and revolt and creates the need for *suppression.*

Thus, in capitalist society we have a democracy that is curtailed, wretched, false; a democracy only for the rich, for the minority. The dictatorship of the proletariat, the period of transition to Communism, will for the first time create democracy for the people, for the majority, along with the necessary suppression of the minority—the exploiters. Communism alone is capable of giving really complete democracy, and the more complete it is the more quickly will it become unnecessary and wither away of itself.

In other words: under capitalism we have the state in the proper sense of the word, that is, a special machine for the suppression of one class by another, and, what is more, of the majority by the minority. Naturally, to be successful, such an undertaking as the systematic suppression of the exploited majority by the exploiting minority calls for the utmost ferocity and savagery in the work of suppressing, it calls for seas of blood through which mankind has to wade in slavery, serfdom and wage labor.

Furthermore, during the *transition* from capitalism to Communism, suppression is *still* necessary; but it is now the suppression of the exploiting minority by the exploited majority. A special apparatus, a special machine for suppression, the "state," is *still* necessary, but this is now a transitional state; it is no longer a state in the proper sense of the word; for the suppression of the minority of exploiters by the majority of the wage slaves of *yesterday* is comparatively so easy, simple and natural a task that it will entail far less bloodshed than the suppression of the risings of slaves, serfs or wage laborers, and it will cost mankind far less. And it is compatible with the extension of democracy to such an overwhelming majority of the population that the need for a *special machine* of suppression will begin to disappear. The exploiters are naturally unable to suppress the people without a highly complex machine for performing this task: but *the people* can suppress the exploiters even with a very simple "machine," almost without a "machine," without a special apparatus, by the simple *organization of the armed masses* (such as the Soviets of Workers' and Soldiers' Deputies, let us remark, anticipating somewhat).

Lastly, only Communism makes the state absolutely unnecessary, for there is *nobody* to be suppressed—"nobody" in the sense of a *class*, in the sense of a systematic struggle against a definite section of the population. We are not utopians, and do not in the least deny the possibility and inevitability of excesses on the part of *individual persons,* or the need to suppress *such* excesses. But, in the first place, no special machine, no special apparatus of suppression is needed for this; this will be done by the armed people itself, as simply and as readily as any crowd of civilized people, even in modern society, interferes to put a stop to a scuffle or to prevent a woman from being assaulted. And, secondly, we know that the fundamental social cause of excesses, which consist in the violation of the rules of social intercourse, is the exploitation of the masses, their want and their poverty. With the removal of this chief cause, excesses will inevitably begin to *"wither away."* We do not know how quickly and in what succession, but we know that they will wither away. With their withering away the state will also *wither away.* . . .

The Higher Phase of Communist Society . . .

The economic basis for the complete withering away of the state is such a high stage of development of Communism that the antithesis between mental and physical labor disappears when there, consequently, disappears one of the principal sources of modern *social* inequality—a source, moreover, which cannot on any account be removed immediately by the mere conversion of the means of production into public property, by the mere expropriation of the capitalists.

This expropriation will create *the possibility* of an enormous development of the productive forces. And when we see how incredibly capitalism is already *retarding* this development, when we see how much progress could be achieved on the basis of the level of technique now already attained, we are entitled to say with the fullest confidence that the expropriation of the capitalists will inevitably result in an enormous development of the productive forces of human society. But how rapidly this development will proceed, how soon it will reach the point of breaking away from the division of labor, of doing away with the antithesis between mental and physical labor, of transforming labor into "the prime necessity of life"—we do not and *cannot* know.

That is why we are entitled to speak only of the inevitable withering away of the state, emphasizing the protracted nature of this process and its dependence upon the rapidity of development of the *higher phase* of Communism, and leaving the question of the time required for, or the concrete forms of, the withering away quite open, because there is *no* material for answering these questions.

It will become possible for the state to wither away completely when society adopts the rule: "From each according to his ability, to each according to his needs," i.e., when people have become so accustomed to observing the fundamental rules of social intercourse and when their labor becomes so productive that they will voluntarily work *according to their ability*. "The narrow horizon of bourgeois right," which compels one to calculate with the coldheartedness of a Shylock whether one has not worked half an hour more than somebody else, whether one is not getting less pay than somebody else—this narrow horizon will then be crossed. There will then be no need for society to regulate the quantity of products to be received by each; each will take freely "according to his needs."

TROTSKY: WORLD REVOLUTION

In 1919, the Russian Communists sponsored the formation of the Communist International, which was to serve as the head-quarters of the international proletarian revolution expected to take place momentarily. The concluding manifesto of the First Comintern Congress was written by Leon Trotsky (1879–1940), the former Menshevik who joined the Bolsheviks in 1917 and served as Lenin's second-in-command until the latter's final ill-ness. The Manifesto set the tone of permanent Communist hos-tility not only against the bourgeoisie, but particularly against the democratic Socialists of the "Second International."

MANIFESTO OF THE COMMUNIST INTERNATIONAL

Seventy-two years have passed since the Communist Party announced its program to the world in the form of a Mani-festo written by the greatest teachers of the proletarian revolution, Karl Marx and Friedrich Engels. Even at that time communism, which had barely entered the arena of struggle, was beset by the baiting, lies, hatred, and perse-cution of the possessing classes, who rightly sensed in it their mortal enemy. In the course of those seven decades communism developed along complex paths, periods of stormy advance alternating with periods of decline; it has known successes, but also severe defeats. But essentially the movement proceeded along the path indicated in ad-vance by the Manifesto of the Communist Party. The epoch of final, decisive struggle came later than the apostles of social revolution had expected and hoped. But it has come. We communists, the representatives of the revolu-tionary proletariat of various countries of Europe, America, and Asia, who have gathered in Soviet Moscow, feel and consider ourselves to be the heirs and executors of the cause whose program was announced 72 years ago. Our task is to generalize the revolutionary experience of the working class, to cleanse the movement of the disintegrat-

From Leon Trotsky, *Manifesto of the First World Congress of the Com-munist International*, in Jane Degras, ed., *The Communist International, 1919-1943: Documents* (London, Royal Institute of International Affairs, 1956), pp. 38, 44-47.

ing admixtures of opportunism and social-patriotism, to mobilize the forces of all genuinely revolutionary parties of the world proletariat and thereby facilitate and hasten the victory of the communist revolution throughout the world. . . .

When the financial oligarchy think it advisable to get parliamentary cover for their acts of violence, the bourgeois State has at its disposal for this purpose all the manifold instruments inherited from centuries of class rule and multiplied by all the miracles of capitalist technology—lies, demagogy, baiting, calumny, bribery, and terror.

To demand of the proletariat that like meek lambs they comply with the requirements of bourgeois democracy in the final life-and-death struggle with capitalism is like asking a man fighting for his life against cutthroats to observe the artificial and restrictive rules of French wrestling, drawn up but not observed by his enemy.

In this realm of destruction, where not only the means of production and exchange but also the institutions of political democracy lie in bloody ruins, the proletariat must create its own apparatus, designed first and foremost to bind together the working class and to ensure the possibility of its revolutionary intervention in the further development of mankind. This apparatus is the workers' Soviets. The old parties, the old trade unions, have in the persons of their leaders proved incapable of carrying out, even of understanding, the tasks presented by the new epoch. The proletariat has created a new kind of apparatus, which embraces the entire working class regardless of occupation or political maturity; a flexible apparatus capable of continual renewal and extension, of drawing broader and broader strata into its orbit, opening its doors to the working people in town and country who stand close to the proletariat. This irreplaceable organization of working-class self-government, of its struggle, and later of its conquest of State power, has been tested in the experience of various countries and represents the greatest achievement and mightiest weapon of the proletariat of our time.

In all countries where the masses have wakened to consciousness, Soviets of workers', soldiers', and peasants' deputies will continue to be built. To strengthen the Soviets, to raise their authority, to put them up in opposition to the State apparatus of the bourgeoisie—this is today the most important task of the class-conscious and honest workers of all countries. Through the Soviets the working class can save itself from the disintegration introduced into its midst by the hellish sufferings of war and of hunger, by the violence of the possessing classes and by the treachery of its former leaders. Through the Soviets the working class will be able most surely and easily to come to power in all those countries where the Soviets are able to rally the majority of the working people. Through the Soviets the working class, having conquered power, will manage all spheres of economic and cultural life, as is the case at present in Russia.

The collapse of the imperialist State, from the Tsarist to the most democratic, is proceeding simultaneously with the collapse of the imperialist military system. The multi-millioned armies mobilized by imperialism could stand firm only so long as the proletariat remained obediently under the yoke of the bourgeoisie. The breakdown of national unity means also an inevitable breakdown of the army. This is what happened first in Russia, then in Austria-Hungary and Germany. The same thing may be expected to occur in other imperialist States. The revolt of the peasant against the landlord, of the worker against the capitalist, and of both against the monarchical or democratic bureaucracy, inevitably brings in its train the revolt of soldiers against the army command, and subsequently a sharp split between the proletarian and bourgeois elements of the army. The imperialist war, which pitted one nation against another, has passed and is passing over into civil war which pits one class against another.

The outcry of the bourgeois world against civil war and red terror is the most monstrous hypocrisy yet known in the history of political struggle. There would be no civil war if the clique of exploiters who have brought mankind to the very brink of ruin had not resisted every forward

step of the working masses, if they had not instigated conspiracies and assassinations, and summoned armed assistance from without in order to maintain or restore their
thievish privileges.

Civil war is forced on the working class by its arch-
enemies. Unless it renounces itself and its own future,
which is also the future of all mankind, the working class
must give blow for blow. The communist parties, which
never conjure up civil war artificially, try to shorten it as
much as possible whenever with iron necessity it does
break out, to reduce to a minimum the number of victims
and, above all, to assure victory to the proletariat. Hence
arises the necessity of disarming the bourgeoisie in time,
of arming the workers, of creating a communist army to
defend the proletarian power and the inviolability of its
socialist construction. Such is the Red Army of Soviet Russia which arose to defend the conquests of the working
class against all attacks from within and without. The Soviet Army is inseparable from the Soviet State.

Conscious of the world-historical character of their tasks,
the enlightened workers, from the very beginning of their
organized socialist movement, strove for association on an
international scale. The foundation stone was laid in London in 1864 in the shape of the First International. The
Franco-Prussian war, from which the Germany of the Ho-
henzollerns emerged, undermined the First International,
while at the same time it gave an impetus to the development of national workers' parties. In 1889 these parties
came together at a congress in Paris and created the organization of the Second International. But the center of
gravity of the workers' movement during this period remained wholly on national soil, wholly within the framework of national States, founded upon national industry
and confined within the sphere of national parliamentarian-
ism. Decades of reformist organizational activity created
a generation of leaders the majority of whom recognized
in words the program of social revolution but denied it by
their actions; they were bogged down in reformism and in
adaptation to the bourgeois State. The opportunist charac-

ter of the leading parties of the Second International was
finally revealed, and it led to the greatest collapse in world
history at a moment when the march of events demanded
revolutionary methods of struggle from the working-class
parties. If the war of 1870 dealt a blow to the First International, disclosing that there was as yet no resolute
mass power behind its social-revolutionary program, then
the war of 1914 killed the Second International, disclosing
that the working masses, though welded together, were
dominated by parties which had become transformed into
subsidiary organs of the bourgeois State!

This applies not only to the social-patriots who have
today gone over openly to the camp of the bourgeoisie,
who have become their favorite agents and the most reliable hangmen of the working class; it also applies to the
amorphous, unstable socialist center, which is now trying
to re-establish the Second International, that is, to re-establish the narrowness, the opportunism, and the revolutionary
impotence of its leading élites. The Independent Party of
Germany, the present majority of the Socialist Party of
France, the Menshevik group of Russia, the Independent
Labor Party of England, and other groups are actually
trying to fill the place occupied before the war by the old
official parties of the Second International by coming forward, as before, with ideas of compromise and unity, using
all the means at their disposal to paralyze the energy of the
proletariat, to prolong the crisis, and thus make Europe's
calamities even greater. The struggle against the socialist
center is the indispensable premise for the successful struggle against imperialism.

In rejecting the timidity, the lies, and the corruption of
the obsolete official socialist parties, we communists, united
in the Third International, consider that we are carrying
on in direct succession the heroic endeavors and martyr-
dom of a long line of revolutionary generations from Babeuf to Karl Liebknecht and Rosa Luxemburg.*

* Gracchus Babeuf—French proponent of communism, executed in 1797;
Liebknecht and Luxemburg—founders of the German Communist Party,
killed in January, 1919. [Ed.]

If the First International predicted the future course of development and indicated the roads it would take, if the Second International rallied and organized millions of proletarians, then the Third International is the International of open mass struggle, the International of revolutionary realization, the International of action.

The bourgeois world order has been sufficiently lashed by socialist criticism. The task of the international communist party consists in overthrowing that order and erecting in its place the edifice of the socialist order.

We summon the working men and women of all countries to unite under the communist banner under which the first great victories have already been won.

Proletarians of all countries! In the struggle against imperialist savagery, against monarchy, against the privileged estates, against the bourgeois State and bourgeois property, against all kinds and forms of social and national oppression—*Unite!*

Under the banner of workers' Soviets, under the banner of revolutionary struggle for power and the dictatorship of the proletariat, under the banner of the Third International—proletarians of all countries, unite!

TROTSKY: THE STRUGGLE AGAINST
THE BUREAUCRACY

*In 1923 Trotsky was outmaneuvered as successor to Lenin by
other Soviet leaders. Trotsky made his historic mark in a fruit-
less struggle against Stalin, which culminated in Trotsky's exile
from the Soviet Union in 1929. Trotsky's first and clearest public statement of his opposition view was the pamphlet,* The
New Course, *December, 1923.*

THE NEW COURSE

. . . The party must subordinate to itself its own apparatus
without for a moment ceasing to be a centralized organization.

In the debates and articles of recent times, it has been
underlined that "pure," "complete," "ideal" democracy is
not realizable and that in general for us it is not an end in
itself. That is incontestable. But it can be stated with just as
much reason that pure, absolute centralism is unrealizable
and incompatible with the nature of a mass party, and that
it can no more be an end in itself than can the party apparatus. Democracy and centralism are two faces of party
organization. The question is to harmonize them in the most
correct manner, that is, the manner best corresponding to
the situation. During the last period there was no such
equilibrium. The center of gravity wrongly centered in the
apparatus. The initiative of the party was reduced to the
minimum. Thence, the habits and the procedures of leadership, fundamentally contradicting the spirit of revolutionary
proletarian organization. The excessive centralization of the
apparatus at the expense of initiative engendered a feeling
of *uneasiness,* an uneasiness which, at the extremities of the
party, assumed an exceedingly morbid form and was translated, among other things, in the appearance of illegal
groupings directed by elements indubitably hostile to communism. At the same time, the whole of the party disap-
proved more and more of apparatus methods of solving

From Leon Trotsky, *The New Course* (Max Shachtman, translator; New
York, Pioneer Publishers, 1943), pp. 90-95.

questions. The idea, or at the very least the feeling, that bureaucratism threatened to get the party into a blind alley, had become pretty general. Voices were raised to point out the danger. The resolution on the new course is the first official expression of the change that has taken place in the party. It will be realized to the degree that the party, that is, its four hundred thousand members, will want to realize it and will succeed in doing so. . . .

Bureaucratism kills initiative and thus prevents the elevation of the general level of the party. That is its cardinal defect. As the apparatus is made up inevitably of the most experienced and most meritorious comrades, it is upon the political training of the young Communist generations that bureaucratism has its most grievous repercussions. Also, it is the youth, the most reliable barometer of the party, that reacts most vigorously against party bureaucratism. . . .

. . . We, the "elders," we ought to say to ourselves plainly that our generation, which naturally enjoys the leading role in the party, is not *absolutely* guaranteed against the gradual and imperceptible weakening of the revolutionary and proletarian spirit in its ranks if the party were to tolerate the further growth and stabilization of bureaucratic methods which transform the youth into the passive material of education and inevitably create an estrangement between the apparatus and the mass, the old and the young. The party has no other means to employ against this indubitable danger than a serious, profound, radical change of course toward party democracy and the increasingly large flow into its midst of working-class elements. . . .

. . . The renovation of the party apparatus—naturally within the clear-cut framework of the statutes—must aim at replacing the mummified bureaucrats with fresh elements closely linked with the life of the collectivity, or capable of assuring such a link. And before anything else, the leading posts must be cleared out of those who, at the first word of criticism, of objection, or of protest, brandish the thunderbolts of penalties before the critic. The "new course" must begin by making everyone feel that from now on nobody will dare terrorize the party.

It is entirely insufficient for our youth to repeat our formulae. It must conquer the revolutionary formulae, it must
assimilate them, work out its own opinions, its own physi-
ognomy; it must be capable of fighting for its views with
the courage which arises out of the depths of conviction
and independence of character. Out of the party with passive obedience, with mechanical leveling by the authorities,
with suppression of personality, with servility, with career-
ism! A Bolshevik is not merely a disciplined man; he is a
man who in each case and on each question forges a firm
opinion of his own and defends it courageously and independently, not only against his enemies, but inside his own
party. Today, perhaps, he will be in the minority in his organization. He will submit, because it is his party. But
this does not always signify that he is in the wrong. Perhaps he saw or understood before the others did a new
task or the necessity of a turn. He will persistently raise
the question a second, a third, a tenth time, if need be.
Thereby he will render his party a service, helping it meet
the new task fully armed or carry out the necessary turn
without organic upheavals, without factional convulsions.

Yes, our party would be unable to discharge its historic
mission if it were chopped up into factions. That should
not and will not happen. It will not decompose in this way
because, autonomous collectivity that it is, its organism re-
sists it. But it will combat successfully the dangers of factionalism only by developing and consolidating the new
course toward workers' democracy. *Bureaucratism of the
apparatus is precisely one of the principal sources of factionalism.* It ruthlessly represses criticism and drives the
discontentment back into the depths of the organization.
It tends to put the label of factionalism upon any criticism,
any warning. Mechanical centralism is necessarily comple-
mented by factionalism, which is at once a malicious cari-
cature of democracy and a potential political danger. . . .

STALIN: THE DICTATORSHIP OF THE PARTY

Joseph Stalin (born Dzhugashvili, 1879–1953), was selected by Lenin to be General Secretary of the Russian Communist Party in 1922. This position enabled him to take control of the party organization after Lenin's illness and death, and eventually to make himself dictator. Stalin made his first important theoretical statement in 1924, in a series of lectures entitled "Foundations of Leninism," in which his purpose was to discredit Trotsky and justify the power and discipline of the party.

FOUNDATIONS OF LENINISM

In the prerevolutionary period, in the period of more or less peaceful development, when the parties of the Second International were the predominant force in the working-class movement and parliamentary forms of struggle were regarded as the principal forms, the Party neither had nor could have had that great and decisive importance which it acquired afterwards, under conditions of open revolutionary battle. Defending the Second International against attacks made upon it, Kautsky says that the parties of the Second International are instruments of peace and not of war, and that for this very reason they were powerless to take any important steps during the war, during the period of revolutionary action by the proletariat. That is quite true. But what does it mean? It means that the parties of the Second International are unfit for the revolutionary struggle of the proletariat, that they are not militant parties of the proletariat, leading the workers to power, but election machines adapted for parliamentary elections and parliamentary struggle. This, in fact, explains why, in the days when the opportunists of the Second International were in the ascendancy, it was not the Party but its parliamentary group that was the chief political organization of the proletariat. It is well known that the Party at that time was really an appendage and subsidiary of the parliamentary

From Joseph Stalin, "Foundations of Leninism," in Stalin, *Problems of Leninism* (Moscow, Foreign Languages Publishing House, 1940), pp. 72-73, 79-81.

group. It goes without saying that under such circumstances and with such a Party at the helm there could be no question of preparing the proletariat for revolution.

But matters have changed radically with the dawn of the new period. The new period is one of open class collisions, of revolutionary action by the proletariat, of proletarian revolution, a period when forces are being directly mustered for the overthrow of imperialism and the seizure of power by the proletariat. In this period the proletariat is confronted with new tasks, the tasks of reorganizing all Party work on new, revolutionary lines; of educating the workers in the spirit of revolutionary struggle for power; of preparing and moving up the reserves; of establishing an alliance with the proletarians of neighboring countries; of establishing firm ties with the liberation movement in the colonies and dependent countries, etc., etc. To think that these new tasks can be performed by the old Social-Democratic parties, brought up as they were under the peaceful conditions of parliamentarism, is to doom oneself to hopeless despair and inevitable defeat. If, with such tasks to shoulder, the proletariat remained under the leadership of the old parties, it would be completely unarmed. It goes without saying that the proletariat could not consent to such a state of affairs.

Hence the necessity for a new party, a militant party, a revolutionary party, one bold enough to lead the proletarians to the struggle for power, sufficiently experienced to find its bearings amidst the complex conditions of a revolutionary situation, and sufficiently flexible to steer clear of all submerged rocks on the way to its goal.

Without such a party it is useless even to think of overthrowing imperialism and achieving the dictatorship of the proletariat.

This new party is the party of Leninism.

What are the specific features of this new party?

The Party as the vanguard of the working class. The Party must be, first of all, the *vanguard* of the working class. The Party must absorb all the best elements of the working class, their experience, their revolutionary spirit, their selfless devotion to the cause of the proletariat. But in order that it may really be the vanguard, the Party must be armed with revolutionary theory, with a knowledge of the laws of the movement, with a knowledge of the laws of revolution. Without this it will be incapable of directing the struggle of the proletariat, of leading the proletariat. The Party cannot be a real party if it limits itself to registering what the masses of the working class feel and think, if it drags at the tail of the spontaneous movement, if it is unable to overcome the inertness and the political indifference of the spontaneous movement, if it is unable to rise above the momentary interests of the proletariat, if it is unable to elevate the masses to the level of the class interests of the proletariat. The Party must stand at the head of the working class; it must see farther than the working class; it must lead the proletariat, and not follow in the tail of the spontaneous movement. . . .

. . . *The Party as the instrument of the dictatorship of the proletariat.* The Party is the highest form of organization of the proletariat. The Party is the principal guiding force within the class of the proletarians and among the organizations of that class. But it does not by any means follow from this that the Party can be regarded as an end in itself, as a self-sufficient force. The Party is not only the highest form of class association of the proletarians; it is at the same time an *instrument* in the hands of the proletariat *for* achieving the dictatorship where that has not yet been achieved and *for* consolidating and expanding the dictatorship where it has already been achieved. The Party could not have risen so high in importance and could not have overshadowed all other forms of organization of the proletariat, if the latter were not confronted with the problem of power, if the conditions of imperialism, the inevitability of wars, and the existence of a crisis did not demand the concentration of all the forces of the proletariat at one point, the gathering of all the threads of the revolutionary movement into one spot in order to overthrow the bourgeoisie and to achieve the dictatorship of the proletariat. The Proletariat needs the Party first of all as its General

Staff, which it must have for the successful seizure of
power. It need hardly be proved that without a Party
capable of rallying around itself the mass organizations of
the proletariat, and of centralizing the leadership of the entire movement during the progress of the struggle, the
proletariat in Russia could never have established its revolutionary dictatorship.

But the proletariat needs the Party not only to achieve
the dictatorship; it needs it still more to maintain the dictatorship, to consolidate and expand it in order to achieve
the complete victory of Socialism.

"Certainly almost everyone now realizes," says Lenin,
"that the Bolsheviks could not have maintained themselves
in power for two and a half months, let alone for two and
a half years, without the strictest and truly iron discipline
in our Party, and without the fullest and most unreserved
support rendered it by the whole mass of the working class,
that is, by all thinking, honest, self-sacrificing and influential elements in it who are capable of leading or of attract-
ing the backward strata."

Now, what does it mean to "maintain" and "expand" the
dictatorship? It means imbuing the millions of proletarians
with the spirit of discipline and organization; it means
creating among the proletarian masses a cementing force
and a bulwark against the corrosive influences of the petty-
bourgeois elements and petty-bourgeois habits; it means
enhancing the organizing work of the proletarians in re-
educating and remolding the petty-bourgeois strata; it
means helping the masses of the proletarians to educate
themselves as a force capable of abolishing classes and
of preparing the conditions for the organization of Socialist
production. But it is impossible to accomplish all this without a party which is strong by reason of its solidarity and
discipline.

"The dictatorship of the proletariat," says Lenin, "is a
persistent struggle—sanguinary and bloodless, violent and
peaceful, military and economic, educational and adminis-

trative—against the forces and traditions of the old society. The force of habit of millions and tens of millions is a most terrible force. Without an iron party tempered in the struggle, without a party enjoying the confidence of all that is honest in the given class, without a party capable of watching and influencing the mood of the masses, it is impossible to conduct such a struggle successfully."

The proletariat needs the Party for the purpose of achieving and maintaining the dictatorship. The Party is an instrument of the dictatorship of the proletariat.

But from this it follows that when classes disappear and the dictatorship of the proletariat withers away, the Party will also wither away.

The Party as the embodiment of unity of will, incompatible with the existence of factions. The achievement and maintenance of the dictatorship of the proletariat is impossible without a party which is strong by reason of its solidarity and iron discipline. But iron discipline in the Party is inconceivable without unity of will, without complete and absolute unity of action on the part of all members of the Party. This does not mean, of course, that the possibility of contests of opinion within the Party is thereby precluded. On the contrary, iron discipline does not preclude but presupposes criticism and contest of opinion within the Party. Least of all does it mean that discipline must be "blind." On the contrary, iron discipline does not preclude but presupposes conscious and voluntary submission, for only conscious discipline can be truly iron discipline. But after a contest of opinion has been closed, after criticism has been exhausted and a decision has been arrived at, unity of will and unity of action of all Party members are the necessary conditions without which neither Party unity nor iron discipline in the Party is conceivable.

"In the present epoch of acute civil war," says Lenin, "a Communist Party will be able to perform its duty only if it is organized in the most centralized manner, only if iron discipline bordering on military discipline prevails in it, and if its Party center is a powerful and authoritative organ, wielding wide powers and enjoying the universal confidence of the members of the Party."

This is the position in regard to discipline in the Party in the period of struggle preceding the achievement of the dictatorship.

The same, but to an even greater degree, must be said about discipline in the Party after the dictatorship has been achieved.

"Whoever in the least," says Lenin, "weakens the iron discipline of the party of the proletariat (especially during its dictatorship) actually aids the bourgeoisie against the proletariat."

But from this it follows that the existence of factions is incompatible either with the Party's unity or with its iron discipline. It need hardly be proved that the existence of factions leads to the existence of a number of centers, and the existence of a number of centers connotes the absence of one common center in the Party, the breaking up of the unity of will, the weakening and disintegration of discipline, the weakening and disintegration of the dictatorship. . . .

STALIN: THE REVOLUTION OF INDUSTRIALIZATION

In 1929, after he had defeated the Communist opposition factions led by Trotsky (the "Left") and Nikolai Bukharin (the "Right"), Stalin introduced new policies of rapid industrial construction, collectivization of agriculture, and tight totalitarian controls. He adapted the Communist dictatorship to the task of completing the industrialization of Russia which capitalism had not had time to finish.

It soon appeared that the attainment of industrial growth and national power required a revision of the Communist ideal of society. Stalin stated the change frankly in two key speeches in 1931, and Communist policy has since followed this approach.

THE TASKS OF BUSINESS EXECUTIVES

. . . Did we have the "objective" possibility last year for completely fulfilling the plan? Yes, we had. Incontestable facts testify to this. The facts are that in March and April of last year industrial output showed an increase of 31 per cent as compared with the previous year. Why then did we fail to fulfill the plan for the whole year? What prevented it? What was lacking? *The ability to make use of the available possibilities was lacking. The ability to direct the factories, mills and mines properly was lacking.*

We had the first condition: the "objective" possibilities for fulfilling the plan. But we did not have in sufficient degree the second condition: the ability to direct production. And precisely because we lacked the ability to direct the factories properly, the plan was not carried out in full. Instead of 31 to 32 per cent increase we had only 25 per cent.

Of course, a 25 per cent *increase* is a big thing. Not a single capitalist country *increased* its production in 1930, nor are there any that are *increasing* production now. All capitalist countries without exception show a sharp decline

From Joseph Stalin, "The Tasks of Business Executives," pp. 360-361, 364-367, and "New Conditions—New Tasks," pp. 371-373, 378-380, in *Problems of Leninism* (Moscow: Foreign Languages Publishing House, 1940).

in production. Under such circumstances a 25 per cent
increase is a big step forward. But we could have achieved
more. We had all the necessary "objective" conditions for
this.

Thus, what guarantee is there that what happened last
year will not happen again this year; that the plan will be
carried out in full; that proper use will be made of the
available possibilities; that your promise will not to some
extent remain a promise on paper?

In the history of states and countries, in the history of
armies, there have been cases when every opportunity for
success and for victory was on hand, but these opportunities were wasted because the leaders did not see them,
did not know how to make use of them, and the armies
suffered defeat.

Have we all the possibilities that are needed to fulfill the
control figures for 1931?

Yes, we have these possibilities.

What are these possibilities? What are the necessary
factors that make these possibilities real?

First of all, adequate *natural resources* in the country:
iron ore, coal, oil, grain, cotton. Have we these resources?
Yes, we have. We have them in larger quantities than any
other country. Take the Urals, for example, which represent a combination of wealth that cannot be found in any
other country. Ore, coal, oil, grain—what is there not in
the Urals? We have everything in our country, except,
perhaps, rubber. But within a year or two we will have our
own rubber as well. As far as natural resources are concerned we are fully secured. We have even more than
enough.

What else is needed?

A *government* capable and willing to utilize these immense natural resources for the benefit of the people. Have
we such a government? We have. True, our work in utilizing natural resources is sometimes accompanied by friction
among our own executives. For instance, last year the Soviet government had to contend with a certain amount of
struggle over the question of creating a second coal and

metal base, without which we cannot develop further. But we have already overcome these obstacles and shall soon have this base.

What else is needed?

That this government should enjoy the *support* of the vast masses of workers and peasants. Does our government enjoy such support? Yes, it does. You will find no other government in the world that enjoys such support from the workers and peasants as does the Soviet government. There is no need for me to enlarge on the growth of Socialist emulation, the spread of shock work, the campaign for counterplans. All these facts, which clearly demonstrate the support which the vast masses give the Soviet government, are well known. . . .

. . . The underlying cause of wrecking activities is the class struggle. Of course, the class enemy is furiously resisting the Socialist offensive. This alone, however, is not an adequate explanation for the luxuriant growth of wrecking activities.

How is it that sabotage has assumed such wide dimensions? Who is to blame for this? We are to blame. Had we handled the business of industrial management differently, had we started much earlier to learn the technique of the business, to master technique, had we more frequently and efficiently intervened in the management of production, the wreckers could not have done so much damage.

We must ourselves become experts, masters of the business; we must turn to technical science—such was the lesson life itself was teaching us. But neither the first signal, nor even the second signal, brought about the necessary change. It is time, it is high time that we turned towards technique. It is time we cast aside the old slogan, the obsolete slogan of noninterference in technique, and ourselves become specialists, experts, complete masters in our various lines.

It is frequently asked: Why have we not one-man management? We do not have it and will not have it until we have mastered technique. Until there are among us Bolsheviks a sufficient number of people thoroughly familiar with technique, economics and finance, we will not have real one-man management. You can write as many resolutions as you please, take as many vows as you please, but, unless you master the technique, economics and finance of the mill, factory or mine, nothing will come of it, there will be no one-man management.

Hence, the task is for us to master technique ourselves, to become the masters of the job ourselves. This is the sole guarantee that our plans will be carried out in full, and that one-man management will be established.

This, of course, is no easy matter; but it can certainly be accomplished. Science, technical experience, knowledge, are all things that can be acquired. We may not have them today, but tomorrow we will. The main thing is to have the passionate Bolshevik desire to master technique, to master the science of production. Everything can be achieved, everything can be overcome, if there is a passionate desire to do so.

It is sometimes asked whether it is not possible to slow down the tempo a bit, to put a check on the movement. No, comrades, it is not possible! The tempo must not be reduced! On the contrary, we must increase it as much as is within our powers and possibilities. This is dictated to us by our obligations to the workers and peasants of the U.S.S.R. This is dictated to us by our obligations to the working class of the whole world.

To slacken the tempo would mean falling behind. And those who fall behind get beaten. But we do not want to be beaten. No, we refuse to be beaten! One feature of the history of old Russia was the continual beatings she suffered for falling behind, for her backwardness. She was beaten by the Mongol Khans. She was beaten by the Turkish beys. She was beaten by the Swedish feudal lords. She was beaten by the Polish and Lithuanian gentry. She was beaten by the British and French capitalists. She was beaten by the Japanese barons. All beat her—for her backwardness: for military backwardness, for cultural backwardness, for political backwardness, for industrial backwardness, for agricultural backwardness. She was beaten because to do so was profitable and could be done with impunity. Do you remember the words of the prerevolutionary poet: "You are poor and abundant, mighty and impotent, Mother Russia." These words of the old poet were well learned by those gentlemen. They beat her, saying: "You are abundant," so one can enrich oneself at your expense. They beat her, saying: "You are poor and impotent," so you can be beaten and plundered with impunity. Such is the law of the exploiters—to beat the backward and the weak. It is the jungle law of capitalism. You are backward, you are weak—therefore you are wrong; hence, you can be beaten and enslaved. You are mighty—therefore you are right; hence, we must be wary of you.

That is why we must no longer lag behind.

In the past we had no fatherland, nor could we have one. But now that we have overthrown capitalism and power is in the hands of the working class, we have a fatherland, and we will defend its independence. Do you want our Socialist fatherland to be beaten and to lose its independence? If you do not want this you must put an end to its backwardness in the shortest possible time and develop genuine Bolshevik tempo in building up its Socialist system of economy. There is no other way. That is why Lenin said during the October Revolution: "Either perish, or overtake and outstrip the advanced capitalist countries."

We are fifty or a hundred years behind the advanced countries. We must make good this distance in ten years. Either we do it, or they crush us.

This is what our obligations to the workers and peasants of the U.S.S.R. dictate to us.

But we have other, still more serious and more important obligations. They are our obligations to the world proletariat. They coincide with our obligations to the workers and peasants of the U.S.S.R. But we place them higher. The working class of the U.S.S.R. is part of the world working class. We achieved victory not only as a result of the efforts of the working class of the U.S.S.R., but also thanks to the support of the working class of the world. Without this support we would have been torn to pieces long ago. It is said that our country is the shock-brigade of the proletariat of all countries. This is well said. But this imposes very serious obligations upon us. Why does the international proletariat support us? How did we merit this support? By the fact that we were the first to hurl ourselves into the battle against capitalism, we were the first to establish a working-class state, we were the first to start building Socialism. By the fact that we are doing work which, if successful, will change the whole world and free the entire working class. But what is needed for success? The elimination of our backwardness, the development of a high Bolshevik tempo of construction. We must march forward in such a way that the working class of the whole world, looking at us, may say: "This is my vanguard, this is my shock-brigade, this is my working-class state, this is my fatherland; they are promoting their cause, which is our cause, and they are doing this well; let us support them against the capitalists and spread the cause of the world revolution." Must we not justify the hopes of the world's working class, must we not fulfil our obligations to them? Yes, we must if we do not want utterly to disgrace ourselves.

Such are our obligations, internal and international.

You see, they dictate to us a Bolshevik tempo of development.

I will not say that we have accomplished nothing in regard to economic management during these years. In fact, we have accomplished a good deal. We have doubled our industrial output as compared with the pre-war level. We have created the largest scale agricultural production in the world. But we could have accomplished more had we tried hard during this period really to master the business of production, the technique of production, the financial and economic side of it.

In ten years at most we must make good the distance we are lagging behind the advanced capitalist countries. We have all the "objective" opportunities for this. The only thing lacking is the ability to make proper use of these opportunities. And that depends on us. *Only* on us! It is time we learned to use these opportunities. It is time to put an end to the rotten policy of noninterference in production. It is time to adopt a new policy, a policy adapted to the times—the policy of interfering in everything. If you are a factory manager, then interfere in all the affairs of the factory, look into everything, let nothing escape you, learn and learn again. Bolsheviks must master technique. It is time Bolsheviks themselves became experts. In the period of reconstruction technique decides everything. And a business executive who does not want to study technique, who does not want to master technique, is a joke and not an executive.

It is said that it is hard to master technique. This is not true! There are no fortresses which Bolsheviks cannot capture. We have solved a number of most difficult problems. We have overthrown capitalism. We have assumed power. We have built up a huge Socialist industry. We have turned the middle peasants to the path of Socialism. We have already accomplished what is most important from the point of view of construction. What remains to be done is not so much: to study technique, to master science. And when we have done this we will develop a tempo of which we dare not even dream at present. And we can do this if we really want to. . . .

NEW CONDITIONS—NEW TASKS

What is the cause of the heavy turnover of labor power?

The cause is the wrong structure of wages, the wrong wage scales, the "Leftist" practice of wage equalization. In a number of our factories wage scales are drawn up in such a way as to practically wipe out the difference between skilled labor and unskilled labor, between heavy work and light work. The consequence of wage equalization is that the unskilled worker lacks the incentive to become a skilled worker and is thus deprived of the prospect of advancement; as a result he feels himself a "sojourner" in the factory, working only temporarily so as to earn a little and then go off to "seek his fortune" elsewhere. The consequence of wage equalization is that the skilled worker is obliged to wander from factory to factory until he finds one where his skill is properly appreciated.

Hence the "general" drift from factory to factory; hence the heavy turnover of labor power.

In order to put an end to this evil we must abolish wage equalization and discard the old wage scales. In order to put an end to this evil we must drawn up wage scales that will take into account the difference between skilled labor and unskilled labor, between heavy work and light work. We cannot tolerate a situation where a rolling-mill hand in a steel mill earns no more than a sweeper. We cannot tolerate a situation where a railway locomotive driver earns only as much as a copying clerk. Marx and Lenin said that the difference between skilled labor and unskilled labor would exist even under Socialism, even after classes had been abolished; that only under Communism would this difference disappear and that, therefore, even under Socialism "wages" must be paid according to work performed and not according to needs. But the equalitarians among our business executives and trade union officials do not agree with this and believe that under our Soviet system this difference has already disappeared. Who is right, Marx and Lenin, or the equalitarians? We must take it that it is Marx and Lenin who are right. But if that is so, it follows that whoever draws up wage scales on the "principle" of wage equalization, without taking into account the difference between skilled labor and unskilled labor, breaks with Marxism, breaks with Leninism.

In every industry, in every factory, in every department of a factory, there is a leading group of more or less skilled workers who must first of all, and particularly, be retained in industry if we really want to secure for the factories a permanent personnel. These leading groups of workers are the chief link in production. By retaining them in the factory, in the department, we can retain the whole personnel and put an end to the heavy turnover of labor power. But how can we retain them in the factories? We can retain them only by promoting them to higher positions, by raising the level of their wages, by introducing a system of payment that will give the worker his due according to qualification. And what does promoting them to higher positions and raising their wage level imply? It implies, apart from everything else, opening up prospects for the unskilled worker and giving him a stimulus to rise higher, to rise to the category of a skilled worker. You know yourselves that we now need hundreds of thousands and even millions of skilled workers. But in order to get skilled workers we must give the unskilled worker a stimulus and prospect of advancement, of rising to a higher position. And the more boldly we do this the better; for this is the principal means of putting an end to the heavy labor turnover. To economize in this matter would be criminal, it would be going against the interests of our Socialist industry. . . .

We can no longer manage with the very small engineering, technical and administrative staffs with which we managed formerly. It follows that the old centers for training engineering and technical forces are no longer adequate, that we must create a number of new centers—in the Urals, in Siberia and in Central Asia. We must now ensure the supply of three times, five times the number of engineering, technical and administrative forces for industry if we seriously intend to carry out the program of the Socialist industrialization of the U.S.S.R.

But we do not need just *any* kind of administrative, engineering and technical forces. We need *such* administrative, engineering and technical forces as are capable of understanding the policy of the working class of our country, are capable of assimilating that policy and are ready to carry it out conscientiously. And what does this mean? This means that our country has entered a phase of development in which the *working class must create its own industrial and technical intelligentsia*, one that is capable of upholding the interests of the working class in production as the interests of the ruling class.

No ruling class has managed without its own intelligentsia. There are no grounds for believing that the working class of the U.S.S.R. can manage without its own industrial and technical intelligentsia.

The Soviet government has taken this fact into account and has opened wide the doors of all the higher educational institutions in every branch of national economy to members of the working class. You know that tens of thousands of working-class and peasant youths are now attending the higher educational institutions. Whereas formerly, under capitalism, the higher educational institutions were the monopoly of the scions of the rich—today, under the Soviet system, the working class and peasant youth predominate in these institutions. There is no doubt that our educational institutions will soon be turning out thousands of new technicians and engineers, new commanders for our industries.

But that is only one side of the matter. The other side is that the industrial and technical intelligentsia of the working class will be recruited not only from among those who have passed through the institutions of higher learning, but also from among practical workers in our factories, from the skilled workers, from among the working-class cultural forces in the mills, factories and mines. The initiators of Socialist emulation, the leaders of shock-brigades, practical inspirers of labor enthusiasm, organizers of work in the various sections of our construction—such is the new stratum of the working class that, together with the comrades who have passed through the institutions of higher learning, must form the core of the intelligentsia of the working class, the core of the commanding personnel of our industry. The task is not to discourage these comrades who show initiative, but boldly to promote them to commanding positions; to give them the opportunity to display their organizing abilities and the opportunity to supplement their knowledge; to create suitable conditions for them to work in, not stinting money for this purpose.

Among these comrades not a few are non-Party people. But that should not prevent us from boldly promoting them to leading positions. On the contrary, it is particularly these non-Party comrades who must receive our special attention, who must be promoted to commanding positions so that they may see for themselves that the Party appreciates capable and gifted workers. Some comrades think that only Party members may be placed in leading positions in the mills and factories. This is the reason why they not infrequently shove aside non-Party comrades who possess ability and initiative and promote Party members instead, although they are less capable and show no initiative. Needless to say, there is nothing more stupid and reactionary than such a "policy," so-called. It need hardly be proved that such a policy can only discredit the Party and repel the non-Party workers from it. Our policy is by no means to transform the Party into an exclusive caste. Our policy is to create an atmosphere of "mutual confidence," of "mutual control" (*Lenin*) between Party and non-Party workers. One of the reasons why our Party is strong among the working class is that it pursues such a policy.

Hence, the task is *to see to it that the working class of the U.S.S.R. has its own industrial and technical intelligentsia. . . .*

KHRUSHCHEV: THE PROMISE OF A COMMUNIST FUTURE

Nikita Khrushchev (1894–   ) became First Secretary of the Communist Party of the Soviet Union after Stalin's death in 1953, and by 1957 he had become (for the time) the unchallenged leader of the Soviet Union. Khrushchev continued to stress industrial progress; in 1961, in his new Program for the Communist Party, he declared that Soviet Russia had begun the "transition to Communism" long ago predicted by Marx. Khrushchev's policies and doctrines for the most part survived his personal fall in 1964.

ON THE PROGRAM OF THE COMMUNIST PARTY

Comrades, the new Program is a new milestone in the history of our Party and of Soviet society as a whole. Each of our Party Programs corresponds to a definite historical stage in the country's development. Yet all our Programs are interlinked. Taken as components of a single whole, they form an integral Marxist-Leninist theory of socialist revolution, of socialist and communist construction, a theory confirmed by experience. The Programs of the Party may be compared to a three-stage rocket.* The first stage wrested our country away from the capitalist world, the second propelled it to socialism, and the third is to place it in the orbit of communism. It is a wonderful rocket, comrades! (*Stormy applause.*) It follows the exact course charted by the great Lenin and by our revolutionary theory, and is powered by the greatest of all energies—the energy of the builders of communism. (*Applause.*)

What are the main features of the draft Program?

The main thing is that *it is a concrete, scientifically substantiated program for the building of communism.* The draft shows clearly how the bright edifice of communism

From N. S. Khrushchev, "On the Programme of the Communist Party of the Soviet Union," in *The Road to Communism: Documents of the 22nd Congress of the Communist Party of the Soviet Union*, Oct. 17-31, 1961 (Moscow, Foreign Languages Publishing House, 1961), pp. 187-190, 192-196.
* Reference to the Programs of 1903 and 1919, as well as 1961. [Ed.]

is to be erected. We see how it should be built, how it looks from within and without, what kind of people will live in it, and what they will do to make it still more comfortable and attractive. We can proudly tell those who want to know what communism is: "Read our Party Program." (*Prolonged applause.*)

The draft Program marks *a new stage in the development of the revolutionary theory of Marx, Engels and Lenin.* The Program furnishes an explicit answer to all the basic questions of the theory and practice of the struggle for communism and to the key questions of present-day world development. The Twentieth and Twenty-First congresses of the C.P.S.U., which introduced much that was new in principle into the solution of the fundamental issues of Party life and the life of Soviet society, and into the analysis of the processes of world development, have been of enormous, truly historic importance in the drafting of the Program. It would have been much harder for us to work out such a Program if there had been no Twentieth and Twenty-First congresses of the C.P.S.U.

The spirit and contents of the draft reflect *the unity and indivisibility of Marxist-Leninist theory and the practice of communist construction.* The Program defines concrete tasks in industry, agriculture, development of the state, science and culture and in communist education. Comrades, just think of the heights the Soviet people have scaled, if they can chart the perspective of social development for so considerable a historical period.

The third Party Program is a program of the whole Soviet people. When the Party was adopting its first Program it was followed by small groups of politically conscious workers. When it was adopting its second Program it was followed by the working class and the bulk of the working peasantry. Now it is followed by the whole Soviet people. Our people accepted the Party Program as their own cause, as the greatest purpose of their lives. (*Prolonged applause.*)

The new Program signifies a full realization in practice of the Party slogan, "Everything for the sake of man, for the benefit of man." It gives predominance to matters concerning the further improvement of the people's material well-being and culture, the flowering of the human personality. And that is as it should be. The Bolsheviks hoisted the flag of revolution in order to make the life of the working people joyous and happy. The third Party Program ushers in a period when all the difficulties and hardships borne by the Soviet people in the name of their great cause will be rewarded a hundredfold.

The draft Program proceeds from the new international conditions: *Communism is being built not in a capitalist encirclement, but under the conditions created by the existence of a world socialist system, the increasing superiority of the socialist forces over those of imperialism, of the forces of peace over those of war.* The imperialist countries naturally strive to impede the economic and social progress of the Soviet land in every way, forcing it to incur defense expenditures. If this were not so, our rates of development would be still higher. However, as the forces of socialism increase and world imperialism grows weaker, more favorable conditions will arise for our economic and cultural development.

Our Program is imbued with the spirit of socialist internationalism. Lenin's Party has always honorably fulfilled its obligations with respect to its brothers abroad. In October 1917 it brought the dawn of liberation to the world. It erected the beacon of socialism, and all peoples can see it. That beacon illumines their way towards the new social system. Lenin's Party will bear aloft the banner of internationalism in the future as well. The Party now considers it its prime internationalist duty to build communism in a brief space of history. (*Applause.*)

The draft Program is *a document of true communist humanism; it is imbued with the ideas of peace and fraternity among nations.* We place the continuously expanding might of our country at the service of peace and mankind's progress. When the Soviet Union will have become the first industrial power, when the socialist system will have fully become the decisive factor of world development, and when the peace forces the world over will have grown still greater, the scales will tilt once and for all in favor of the forces of peace and the barometer of the international weather will show: "Clear. The menace of world war is gone never to return." (*Prolonged applause.*) . . .

. . . The draft Program gives the following definition of communism:

"Communism is a classless social system with one single form of public ownership of the means of production and full social equality of all members of society; under it, the all-round development of people will be accompanied by the growth of the productive forces through continuous progress in science and technology; all the springs of collective wealth will flow more abundantly, and the great principle 'From each according to his ability, to each according to his needs' will be implemented. Communism is a highly organized society of free, socially conscious working people in which public self-government will be established, a society in which labor for the good of society will become the prime, vital requirement of everyone, a necessity recognized by one and all, and the ability of each person will be employed to the greatest benefit of the people."

Let me go into some of the aspects in the description of communist society. Communism implies highly-organized production centralized on the scale of society as a whole and managed along the broadest democratic lines. Communist society is not an association of self-contained, autarkic economic organisms. By no means. Communist society, more than any other, will need unified economic planning, organized distribution of labor and regulation of working time. The need of this springs from the demands presented by the development of the productive forces, from the far-reaching interrelation of the various branches of economy, the interests of continuous technical progress and from the communist principles of distribution and consumption. Development of the communist economy is impossible, unless the entire people participate most actively in the management of production.

For the first time, the draft elaborates upon the concrete ways and means of effecting the great communist slogan, "From each according to his ability, to each according to his needs." It is a proper combination of material labor incentives and increasing distribution through public funds that leads up to the implementation of the principles of communist equality.

Some people picture living conditions under communism wrongly and narrowmindedly. They grasp at just the second part of the formula, "according to needs," and reason something like this: "Under communism you work if you wish, or drift from the Far East to the west, and from the west to the south if you wish; you'll be provided according to needs all the same." A big spoon is all they are equipping themselves with for communism. (*Laughter. Applause.*)

We have to disappoint them from the very outset. Their notion has nothing in common with communism. Communist society will have the most advanced technology, the most advanced and best organized production, the most advanced machinery. But it will be people that operate the machines. Machines are dead things, unless there is a man to operate them. Thoroughness, good organization and discipline are therefore a golden rule, an obligatory standard of behavior for every workingman. He will not be made to perform his duties by the goad of hunger, as under capitalism; he will perform them consciously and of his own free will. Everyone will be conscious of the duty to contribute his labor to the creation of both the material and spiritual blessings. All Soviet people must work so well as to be able to say, when the bright edifice of communism is built: I have done my bit for it as well.

The classics of Marxism-Leninism emphasized that communism is not fenced off by a wall from socialism, that communism and socialism are two phases of one and the same socioeconomic formation, distinguished from one another by the degree of economic development and the maturity of social relations.

Socialism does not develop on its own foundation. For all its immense achievements of world historic significance, in many respects—the economic, legal and moral, and in the consciousness of men—it still bears an imprint of the old system, from which it has emerged. Communism is a higher and more perfect stage of social life, and can develop only after socialism is fully consolidated. Under communism all the aftereffects of the capitalist system will be completely eliminated.

The fact that communism develops on its own foundation predetermines the distinctive features of its construction. The transition from capitalism to socialism is effected under conditions of class struggle. It involves a radical breakup of social relations, a sweeping social revolution and the establishment of the dictatorship of the proletariat. On the other hand, the transition to communism proceeds in the absence of any exploiting classes, when all members of society—workers, peasants and intellectuals—have a vested interest in the victory of communism, and work for it consciously. It is natural therefore that the building of communism is effected by the most democratic methods, by way of improving and developing social relations, with due account of the departure of the old forms of life and the appearance of new forms, of their interlacement and mutual influence. Society will no longer experience the difficulties induced by class struggle within the country. All this will serve to accelerate the rates of social development in the period of transition to communism.

The historical limits of the draft Program are 20 years. Why did we set this term? When the draft Program was being discussed, some comrades wondered whether the time allocated to the task was not too long. No, comrades. To prepare society for the establishment of the principles of communism we have to develop the productive forces enormously and create an abundance of material and spiritual values. And that takes a certain amount of time. The bowl of communism is a bowl of abundance, and it

must always be full. Everyone must contribute his bit to
it, and everyone must take from it. It would be a fatal
error to decree the introduction of communism before
all the necessary conditions for it have matured. If we
were to proclaim that we introduce communism when the
bowl is still far from full, we would be unable to take from
it according to needs. In that case we would only discredit
the ideas of communism, disrupt the initiative of the working people and retard the advance to communism. We base
ourselves on strictly scientific estimates, which indicate that
we shall, in the main, have built a communist society within 20 years. (*Prolonged applause.*)

What does it mean to build communism in the main?
It means that:

in the *economic* sphere the material and technical basis
of communism will be created; the economy of the Soviet
Union will surpass that of the most developed capitalist
countries and move into first place for production per head
of the population, the world's highest living standard will
be ensured and all the conditions created to attain an
abundance of material and cultural values;

in the sphere of *social* relations the still existing remnants of distinctions between classes will be eliminated;
classes will fuse into a classless society of communist
working people; the essential distinctions between town
and country, and then between physical and mental labor,
will, in the main, be eradicated; there will be greater economic and ideological community among nations; the features will develop of the man of communist society, a man
harmoniously combining ideological integrity, broad education, moral purity and physical perfection;

in the *political* sphere all citizens will participate in the
administration of public affairs, and society will prepare
itself for the full implementation of the principles of communist self-government through a most extensive development of socialist democracy.

PART THREE

VARIETIES OF COMMUNISM

From 1917 until after the Second World War, the Soviet Union was (apart from its satellite Outer Mongolia) the world's only Communist country. Communists in other countries were compelled to accept the Soviet version of Communism or be expelled from the movement. But the success of Communist revolutionaries in the parts of Eastern Europe and the Far East that had been occupied by Germany and Japan during the war made it possible for new, independent Communist governments to take power. While it was easy for the Soviet Union to control the countries occupied by the Red Army, the government established in Yugoslavia by Josip Broz Tito and his Communist-led guerrilla Partisans was another matter. In 1948 Stalin expelled Yugoslavia from the Communist movement in the hope that Tito would fall, but the Yugoslav Communists asserted their independence and began to work out their own interpretation of Marxism-Leninism.

On a larger scale the same thing happened in the late 1950's and early 1960's, when the new Communist dictatorship in China began to challenge the Soviet leadership of the international Communists. The Chinese Communists, like the Yugoslavs, had come to power largely through their own efforts, after a long history of guerrilla warfare under the leadership of Mao Tse-tung. By the 1960's, they were criticizing the Soviet Union and Khrushchev in the same way that Lenin and the radical Marxists had attacked the Mensheviks and the "revisionists." The Russians replied by charging the Chinese with warlike "adventurism." Underlying the schism between China and Russia was the need for some strong authority to interpret Marxism and justify current Communist practices, coupled with the refusal of the Russians and the Chinese to accept each other's authority in this matter. The result of the controversy, however, was to weaken all central authority in the Communist movement and to permit the rise of "polycentrism."

A new gain for the movement was made with the establishment of another variety of Communism in Cuba, through the conversion of a successful nationalist revolutionary, Fidel Castro, to belief in Marxism-Leninism. Castro's choice was symptomatic of the emotional attraction of Marxism for revolutionary nationalists in the underdeveloped countries, whether or not they have a proletariat to lead. Cuba may represent the future dilemma of Communism—the further it succeeds in new areas, the more difficult it may be to keep the followers of Marxism-Leninism united in a single movement.

MAO TSE-TUNG: THE GUERRILLA REVOLUTION

Mao Tse-tung (1893–   ) came from a family of Chinese provincial gentry and typifies the attraction of Marxism for the educated Asian. He gained control of the Chinese Communist Party in the 1930's, contrary to the wishes of the Russians, by organizing successful guerrilla warfare among the peasants, while the urban Communists were being suppressed by the Nationalist government of Chiang Kai-shek. In 1936, Mao outlined the principles of guerrilla war which guided his successful struggle against the Japanese and then against the Chinese Nationalists (the "Kuomintang"), as well as subsequent Communist movements in Southeast Asia.

STRATEGIC PROBLEMS OF CHINA'S REVOLUTIONARY WAR

II. THE CHINESE COMMUNIST PARTY AND CHINA'S REVOLUTIONARY WAR

China's revolutionary war, which began in 1924, has passed through two stages, *i.e.*, the stage of 1924–27 and the stage of 1927–36; from now on it will enter the stage of the national anti-Japanese revolutionary war. The revolutionary war in all the three stages has been and will be led by the Chinese proletariat and its party, the Chinese Communist Party. The chief enemies in China's revolutionary war are imperialism and the feudal forces. Although the Chinese bourgeoisie may take part in the revolutionary war on certain historical occasions, yet owing to its selfish character and its lack of political and economic independence, it is neither willing nor able to lead China's revolutionary war to complete victory. The masses of the Chinese peasantry and of the urban petty bourgeoisie are willing to take part actively in the revolutionary war and to bring about its complete victory. They are the main forces in the revolutionary war, yet small-scale production,

From Mao Tse-tung, *Strategic Problems of China's Revolutionary War* (Peking, Foreign Languages Press, 1954), pp. 22-23, 34-39, 56-59.

which is their characteristic and limits their political outlook (a section among the unemployed being imbued with
anarchist ideology), renders them unable to give correct
leadership in the war. Thus, in an era when the proletariat
has already appeared on the political stage, the responsibility of leadership in China's revolutionary war inevitably
falls on the shoulders of the Chinese Communist Party. At
such a time any revolutionary war will certainly end in
defeat if the leadership of the proletariat and the Communist Party is lacking or is forsaken. For of all the social
strata and political groups in semicolonial China only the
proletariat and the Communist Party are the most open-
minded and unselfish, possess the most farsighted political
outlook and the highest organizational quality, and are
also the readiest to learn with an open mind from the
experiences of the advanced proletariat of the world and
its parties as well as to apply what they have learned in
their own undertakings. Hence only the proletariat and
the Communist Party can lead the peasantry, the urban
petty bourgeoisie, and the bourgeoisie, overcome the narrowmindedness of the peasantry and the petty bourgeoisie,
the destructiveness of the unemployed masses, and the
vacillation and lack of thoroughness of the bourgeoisie
(provided no mistake is made in the Communist Party's
policy), and thereby lead the revolution and the war to the
path of victory. . . .

III. CHARACTERISTICS OF CHINA'S
REVOLUTIONARY WAR . . .

What then are the characteristics of China's revolutionary
war?

I think there are four.

The first is that China is a vast semicolonial country
which is unevenly developed both politically and economically, and which has gone through the revolution of
1924–27. . . .

Let us now analyze this characteristic.

The unevenness of political and economic development

in China—the coexistence of a frail capitalist economy and a preponderant semifeudal economy; the coexistence of a few modern industrial and commercial cities and the boundless expanses of stagnant rural districts; the coexistence of several millions of industrial workers on the one hand and, on the other, hundreds of millions of peasants and handicraftsmen under the old regime; the coexistence of big warlords controlling the central government and small warlords controlling the provinces; the coexistence of two kinds of reactionary armies, *i.e.*, the so-called central army under Chiang Kai-shek and the troops of miscellaneous bands under the warlords in the provinces; and the coexistence of a few railway and steamship lines and motor roads on the one hand and, on the other, the vast number of wheelbarrow paths and trails for pedestrians only, many of which are even difficult for them to negotiate.

China is a semicolonial country—the disunity among the imperialist countries has caused the disunity among the various ruling blocs in China. A semicolonial state controlled by several countries is different from a colony controlled by a single country.

China is a vast country—"When the east is still dark, the west is lit up; when night falls in the south, the day breaks in the north"; hence one need not worry about whether there is room enough to move around.

China has gone through a great revolution which has provided us with the seeds of the Red Army, the Chinese Communist Party which leads the Red Army, and the masses who have participated in a revolution.

We have said, therefore, that the first characteristic of China's revolutionary war is that China is a vast semicolonial country which has gone through a revolution and is unevenly developed politically and economically. This characteristic basically determines not only our political strategy and tactics, but also our military strategy and tactics.

The second characteristic is the great strength of the enemy.

What is the situation of the Kuomintang, the enemy of

the Red Army? It is a party that has seized political power and has relatively stabilized it. It has gained the support of the principal counterrevolutionary countries in the world. It has remodeled its army which has thus become different from any other army in Chinese history and, on the whole, similar to the armies of the modern states in the world; its army is supplied much more abundantly with arms and other equipment than the Red Army, and is greater in numerical strength than any army in Chinese history, even than the standing army of any country in the world. There is a world of difference between the Kuomintang army and the Red Army. The Kuomintang controls the key positions or lifelines in the politics, economy, communications and culture of China; its political power is nationwide in character.

The Chinese Red Army is confronted with such a powerful enemy. This is the second characteristic of China's revolutionary war. This characteristic inevitably makes the war waged by the Red Army different in many ways from wars in general, from the civil war in the Soviet Union, and from the Northern Expedition.

The third characteristic is that the Red Army is weak and small.

The Chinese Red Army was born after the failure of the first great revolution, starting as guerrilla units. It finds itself existing not only in a period of reaction in China but in a period of relative political and economic stability in the reactionary capitalist countries in the world.

Our political power is dispersed and isolated in mountainous or remote regions, and is deprived of any outside help. In economic and cultural conditions the revolutionary base areas are more backward than the Kuomintang areas. The revolutionary bases embrace only rural districts and small towns. They were extremely small in the beginning and have not grown much larger since. Moreover, they are often shifted and the Red Army possesses no really consolidated bases.

The Red Army is small in number, its arms are poor,

and its access to food, bedding, clothing and other supplies is extremely difficult.

This characteristic presents a sharp contrast to the preceding one. The strategy and tactics of the Red Army are based on this sharp contrast.

The fourth characteristic is the Communist Party's leadership and the agrarian revolution.

This characteristic is the inevitable result of the first one. It gives rise to the following two features. On the one hand, China's revolutionary war, though taking place in a period of reaction in China and throughout the capitalist world, can yet be victorious because it is led by the Communist Party and supported by the peasantry. Because we have secured the support of the peasantry, our base areas, though small, possess great political power and stand firmly opposed to the political power of the Kuomintang, which encompasses a vast area; in a military sense, this creates colossal difficulties for the attacking Kuomintang troops. The Red Army, though small, has great fighting capacity, because its men under the leadership of the Communist Party have sprung from the agrarian revolution and are fighting for their own interests, and because officers and men are politically united.

On the other hand, our situation contrasts sharply with that of the Kuomintang. Opposed to the agrarian revolution, the Kuomintang is deprived of the support of the peasantry. Despite the great size of its army it cannot arouse the bulk of the soldiers or many of the lower-rank officers, who used to be small producers, to risk their lives voluntarily for its sake. Officers and men are politically disunited and this reduces its fighting capacity. . . .

V. STRATEGIC DEFENSIVE . . .

Military experts of new and rapidly developing imperialist countries like Germany and Japan positively boast of the advantages of strategic offensive and condemn strategic defensive. Such an idea is fundamentally unsuitable for China's revolutionary war. Such military experts point out that the great shortcoming of defense lies in the fact that, instead of gingering up the people, it demoralizes them. But that applies only to countries where class contradictions are sharp and the war benefits only the reactionary ruling strata or the reactionary groups in power. Our case is different. Under the slogan of safeguarding the revolutionary base areas and safeguarding China, we can rally the greatest majority of the people to fight singlemindedly because we are the victims of oppression and aggression. The Red Army of the Soviet Union defeated its enemies also by defensive warfare during the civil war. It not only carried on the war under the slogan of defending the Soviets when the imperialist powers organized the Whites for an onslaught, but also carried out military mobilization under the slogan of defending the capital when the October Uprising was being prepared. All defensive battles in a just war cannot only exercise a lulling influence on the politically alien elements but mobilize the backward sections of the masses to join in the war.

When Marx said that once an armed uprising is started there must not be a moment's pause in the attack, he meant that the masses, having taken the enemy by surprise in an uprising, must not allow the reactionary ruling classes any chance to retain or recover their political power, but must seize this moment to spring a surprise attack on the nation's reactionary ruling forces, and that they must never feel satisfied with the victories they have won, underrate the enemy, relent in their attacks, or hesitate to go forward, lest they should miss the chance of annihilating the enemy and court failure for the revolution. This is correct. This does not mean, however, that we revolutionaries should not adopt defensive measures even when we are already locked in a battle with an enemy stronger than ourselves and are hard pressed by him. Any one who thinks so would be a first-class idiot.

Our past war was on the whole an offensive against the Kuomintang, though militarily it assumed the form of smashing the enemy's campaigns of "encirclement and annihilation."

In military terms, our warfare consists in the alternate adoption of the defensive and the offensive. It makes no difference to us whether our offensive is regarded as following the defensive or preceding it, because the turning point comes when we smash the campaigns of "encirclement and annihilation." It remains a defensive until a campaign of "encirclement and annihilation" is smashed, and then it immediately begins as an offensive; they are but two phases of the same thing, as one campaign of "encirclement and annihilation" of the enemy is closely followed by another. Of the two phases the defensive phase is more complicated and more important than the offensive phase. It involves numerous problems on how to smash the campaign of "encirclement and annihilation." The basic principle is for active defense and against passive defense.

In the civil war, when the Red Army surpasses the enemy in strength, there will no longer be any use for strategic defensive in general. Then our only directive will be strategic offensive. Such a change depends on an over-all change in the relative strength of the enemy and ours. The only defensive measures that remain will be of a partial character.

YUGOSLAVIA: DECENTRALIZED COMMUNISM

The independent Communist policy Tito's Yugoslavia followed after 1948 was formalized a decade later in the Program of the League of the Communists of Yugoslavia (as the Communist Party there had been renamed). The program began with a critique both of capitalism and of Soviet Communism, and then proceeded to defend the Yugoslav practices of national independence and administrative decentralization.

PROGRAM OF THE LEAGUE OF COMMUNISTS OF YUGOSLAVIA

. . . The entire social development in the Soviet Union had to begin with the concentration of all forces on the construction of the material basis of the new society. This was the only way to prevent a restoration of capitalism in the Soviet Union. This general situation, however, required extraordinary efforts and great self-denial of the whole working class and the working people of the Soviet Union. . . .

. . . In this general situation, social development called for an emphasis on the organizing role of the leading forces of society—the Communist Party and the Soviet State—first in the fields of economic life, then in all life of society. This is what led to the great concentration of power in the hands of the state apparatus.

However, this concentration of power in the state apparatus began to be accompanied by bureaucratic-state tendencies, mistakes and deformities in the development of the political system of the state. This, in turn, caused a sharper and more convulsive manifestation of the numerous contradictions typical of the transition period from capitalism to socialism.

In the end, this practice gradually led not only to the

From *Yugoslavia's Way: The Program of the League of the Communists of Yugoslavia* (translated by Stoyan Pribichevich, New York: All-Nations Press, 1958), pp. 42-45, 64-65, 120-122, 129-130, 132-133, 152, 173. Reprinted by permission of the publisher.

ever stronger power of the state but to the rule by one man. This is the practice which produced the "cult of personality" and attempts at its theoretical and ideological justification.

Despite the relentless pressure of the forces of capitalism and imperialism, the Communist Party of the Soviet Union and the Soviet working people managed during Stalin's leadership to preserve the achievements of the October Revolution, to consolidate them through successful industrialization and the raising of the general cultural and technical levels of the country, and to maintain and develop the Soviet Union as a support for all socialist and progressive movements. However, for objective and subjective reasons, Stalin did not oppose the bureaucratic-state tendencies stemming from the great concentration of power in the hands of the state apparatus, from the merging of the Party and state apparatus and from lopsided centralism. On the contrary, he himself became their political and ideological champion.

Along these lines a pragmatist revision of certain fundamental scientific propositions of Marxism-Leninism was carried out, first in the theory of the state and the Party, then in philosophy, political economy and the social sciences generally.

The Marxist-Leninist theory of the dictatorship of the proletariat as a political system of government in a state which is withering away and as an instrument of the struggle of the working class in the process of destroying the economic foundations of capitalism and creating the political and material conditions for a free development of new, socialist relations—this Marxist-Leninist theory was transformed into Stalin's theory of the state which is not withering away, which has to grow ever stronger in all areas of social life. To the apparatus of this state is assigned too big a part in the construction of socialism and in the solution of the inner contradictions of the transition period, a part which sooner or later must begin to obstruct the development of the socialist factors in society and economy.

On the international scene, that is, in certain aspects of the Soviet foreign policy and in relations among the socialist countries, phenomena of this kind also appeared after the Second World War. These showed most strikingly in Stalin's action against socialist Yugoslavia, action unanimously condemned at the Twentieth Congress of the Communist Party of the Soviet Union as obviously contrary to the real interests of socialism.

In resisting this pressure and in fighting for the independence of their country, the Yugoslav Communists and the peoples of Yugoslavia not only fought for their right to free socialist development but contributed to the indispensable fight against state-bureaucratic and other antisocialist deformities in the development of socialism and in the relations among nations which have chosen the socialist path. This resistance, therefore, was socialist and progressive by definition, and precisely for this reason it contributed to the strengthening and advancing of socialism throughout the world.

All these and other well-known negative phenomena and errors caused damage both to international socialism and to socialist construction in the Soviet Union, particularly because they were taken over and repeated by certain socialist countries. They were unable, however, to deform or impede for a length of time the development of socialism in the Soviet Union, because socialist forces in this first country of socialism had so grown and become so strong that they even kept breaking through the barriers of bureaucratism and the "cult of personality.". . .

. . . Every aspect of ideological monopoly that hampers free socialist development in socialist countries is a brake on international socialism in general. For this reason, the League of the Communists of Yugoslavia regards as particularly useful today the creation of such forms of international cooperation as would on the broadest possible basis unite efforts toward solution of the common practical problems of peace and of the struggle for, and the building of, socialism.

The interest of further socialist development demands free, socialist, democratic relations among the parties of the socialist countries. In the struggle for the victory of socialism, the working class of one country or another may for a certain period of time be the standard-bearer, may stand in the front ranks or have a superior material force at its disposal. But this does not mean that it thus acquires a monopoly position in the labor movement, least of all in ideology. Past experience has shown—and it is even clearer today—that cooperation in the labor movement is possible only among equals. . . .

To proclaim the path and form of the socialist development of any country as the only correct ones is nothing but dogma, obstructing the process of the socialist transformation of the world. The general aims of socialism are common, but the tempo and forms of the movement of society toward these aims are and must be different, depending on the concrete conditions in individual countries or parts of the world. Consequently, freedom of internal socialist development and absence of any imposition of various forms, noninterference in the internal life and progress of various movements, and a free and equal exchange of experience and socialist theoretical thought should be the basic principle of mutual relations among socialist countries and socialist movements. . . .

Assigning an indispensable and important role to the state in the first stages of socialist construction, and also aware of statist deformation which this role may cause in the development of socialist relations, the Yugoslav Communists believe that the state, that is, its administrative apparatus and measures, are not at all the main instrument of socialist construction and solution of the inner contradictions of socialist development. The state apparatus cannot be the decisive, permanent and all-embracing factor in the development of new social relations. The Yugoslav Communists must not, nor do they wish to, become a power through the use of the state apparatus instead of through the working class and working people. Only the social and economic interest of the working class, of the working people who produce with the social means of production, and socialist consciousness based on that interest, can be the basic, permanent motive power of social progress.

The Communists do not renounce their leading social role. Social consciousness plays the decisive part in the solution of the contradictions of socialist development. But the leading socialist forces can be victorious only if they act in accordance with the objective laws of development and with the needs of society in general; and in particular, if they act in accordance with the social and economic interests of the working class, that is, the working people who produce with the social means of production.

In the struggle for further strengthening of socialism, the Communists must constantly verify their political line through their increasing responsibility to the broad masses of the working people. Taught by practice and by contradictions which appear in socialist development, they must educate the working masses so that these may be able increasingly, more and more directly and independently, to manage society, think like socialists and act in practice like socialists, until each individual citizen learns how to manage the affairs of the social community. . . .

Simultaneously, the Communists will continue the struggle for keeping key positions of state authority in firm revolutionary hands—positions on which depend further development of socialist society and defense of that society against the various internal and foreign anti-socialist forces. The great socialist, democratic, humane and peaceful goals that the Yugoslav socialist society has set itself can be achieved most quickly and least painfully if the enemies of socialism are allowed no opportunity to bring obstacles and disturbances into our internal social life. . . .

Social ownership of the means of production was put into practice in Yugoslavia through a revolutionary transformation. It covers all means of production except those used in personal labor of peasants and craftsmen. Social ownership of the means of production in Yugoslavia has not only completely liquidated private capitalist ownership; it has become a firm foundation and guarantee of such social relations in production where conditions of any ownership monopoly are gradually eliminated. This means elimination, also, of any economic and political monopoly—of any monopoly by individuals and of any monopoly by the socialist state.

The actual social substance of this process consists in the development of self-management of producers in production, in self-government of the working people in the Commune, District, Republic and Federation, and in a clear delimitation of the rights and duties of all these organs. . . .

Yugoslavia has carried out a radical agrarian reform finally limiting individual holdings to 24.71 acres of arable land. This substantially restricts the possibility of capitalist tendencies to assert themselves in private agricultural production.

Considering that land holdings in Yugoslavia are almost exclusively small or medium-sized, the League of the Communists believes that the process of socialization of land will not consist in a forced general nationalization or other similar means but primarily in socialization of agricultural production based on the increasingly stronger forces of production in the economy, and especially in agriculture; in a gradual socialist transformation of the village; in uniting the peasants through cooperatives or in cooperation of the peasants with the social sector of agricultural production. This cooperation is in the first place based on the use of the means of modern large-scale agricultural production, which can be exclusive social property. . . .

The League of the Communists of Yugoslavia believes that the right of individual ownership by citizens of various objects of consumption and use, on which a more varied and more comfortable life of citizens depends, is also an essential personal right and incentive to creative personal initiative.

The prerequisite of the socialist character and scope of

the right to individual ownership is that it does not become a source of personal enrichment by exploiting others, that it does not stem from any special social privilege, that it does not restrict others in enjoying the same right—that, in a word, it returns the individual to society, no longer confining him within the bounds of selfishness and isolation.

The source of individual ownership must be work. Such individual ownership is not abolished in socialism. It must be protected and continuously expanded, because socialism as a whole aims not only at general social progress but also at personal happiness of man. In this sense, a constant inner striving to satisfy as much as possible human needs, activities, tastes, desires, is peculiar to socialism. . . .

The experience of Yugoslavia and of a number of other countries shows that over-all economic plans, no matter how "perfect," cannot exhaust innumerable possibilities, forms or incentives afforded by the spontaneous development of economic forces. Therefore the economic system and plan must not abolish that indispensable degree of independence of the working man, enterprise or other social-economic units without which no conscious initiative is possible and without which man ceases to be creator. They must not suppress either the individual or the collective material interest of the producers in production and work, that is, their constant striving for a higher degree of material welfare, which is one of the essential motive powers of their activity. . . .

The Communists will pay particular attention to the development of Workers' Councils. Workers' Councils are democratic economic-political organs of social self-management through which direct producers independently manage enterprises and take a decisive part in the development of the forces of production—within a single coordinated social economic plan and in accordance with the general interests of the community, expressed in a single coordinated economic system. The motive power of the activity of the direct producers in Workers' Councils, aimed at more productive labor and faster development of the forces of production, is their desire continuously to improve their living conditions and the general material standard of the social community through better individual work, better operation of the enterprise and faster general economic progress of the social community; and to develop freely their individual creative abilities and inclinations, in harmony with the general interests of the working people.

Workers' Councils are neither representatives of the owner nor the collective owner of the means of production. They manage the means of production on behalf of the social community and in their work are stimulated by their own material and moral-political aspirations. Just for this reason, they are the most suitable social-economic instrument of struggle against both bureaucratism and selfish individualism.

CASTRO: FROM NATIONALISM
TO COMMUNISM

Fidel Castro (1925–   ) became the leader of a new revolu-
tionary government in Cuba on January 1, 1959, following a
campaign of guerrilla warfare against the dictatorship of Ful-
gencia Batista. Though Castro was, as a typical Latin-American
intellectual, acquainted with Marxism, he did not belong to the
Communist Party—or receive Communist support—until after he
had taken power. Then the pressure of revolutionary events,
the hostility of the United States, and the blandishments of the
Soviet Union and local Cuban Communists persuaded him that
he had really been a Marxist-Leninist all along. In a television
speech in December 1961, Castro declared his ideological com-
mitment and outlined his plan for a Leninist-type party.

ON MARXISM-LENINISM

I consider myself more revolutionary today than I was
even on the first of January [1959]. Was I a revolutionary
on the first of January? Yes, I believe I was a revolutionary
on the first of January. That is, all of the ideas I have today I had on the first of January.

Now then, am I at this moment a man who has studied
thoroughly all of the political philosophy of the Revolution, the entire history? No, I have not studied it thoroughly.
Of course, I am absolutely convinced and have the intention—an intention we all ought to have—to study. Recently,
while looking through some books up there in the capital,
I found that when I was a student I had read up to page
370 of *Capital*. That's as far as I got. When I have the
time, I plan to continue studying Karl Marx's *Capital*.

In my student years I had studied the Communist Manifesto and selected works of Marx, Engels and Lenin. Of
course, it is very interesting to reread now the things I
read at that time. Well, now, do I believe in Marxism? I
believe absolutely in Marxism! Did I believe on the first of
January? I believed on the first of January. Did I believe

From *Fidel Castro Speaks on Marxism-Leninism* (New York, Fair Play for
Cuba Committee), p. 46-47, 49, 63-65, 72-73.

on the 26th of July?* I believed on the 26th of July! Did I understand it as I do today, after almost ten years of struggle? No, I did not understand it as I do today. Comparing what I understood then with what I understand today, there is a great difference. Did I have prejudices? Yes, I had prejudices on the 26th of July, yes. Could I have been called a thoroughgoing revolutionary on the 26th of July? No, I could not have been called a thoroughgoing revolutionary. Could I have been called a thoroughgoing revolutionary on the first of January? No, I could have been called almost a thoroughgoing revolutionary. Could I be called a thoroughgoing revolutionary today? That would mean that I feel satisfied with what I know and, of course, I am not satisfied. Do I have any doubt about Marxism and do I feel that certain interpretations were wrong and have to be revised? No, I do not have the slightest doubt!

What occurs to me is precisely the opposite: the more experience we gain from life, the more we learn what imperialism is—and not by word, but in the flesh and blood of our people—the more we have to face up to that imperialism; the more we learn about imperialist policies throughout the world, in South Vietnam, in the Congo, in Algeria, in Korea, everywhere in the world; the more we dig deeper and uncover the bloody claws of imperialism, the miserable exploitation, the abuse they commit in the world, the crimes they commit against humanity, the more, in the first place, we feel sentimentally Marxist, emotionally Marxist, and the more we see and discover all the truths contained in the doctrine of Marxism. The more we have to face the reality of a revolution and the class struggle, and we see what the class struggle really is, in the setting of a revolution, the more convinced we become of all of the truths Marx and Engels wrote and the truly ingenious interpretations of scientific socialism Lenin made.

The more we read today, with the experience, the load of experience we have, in those books, the more convinced we become of their inspired vision, of the foresight they had. . . .

* 1953, date of Castro's first abortive coup. [Ed.]

But it wasn't enough that the European labor movement had a revolutionary theory; this theory needed interpretation and so there came a period when the influence of nonrevolutionary thought, of bourgeois thinking and bourgeois ideology tried to distort Marx's thought. What is Lenin's great merit? Well, simply that he takes Marx's thought, defends it against all mystification, against all forms of revisionism, against all of the revisions and changes they wanted to make in the thinking of Marx. Armed only with theory, he forms a party, struggles within that party against all petty-bourgeois currents, against all nonrevolutionary currents, triumphs over these currents in the party and, with a revolutionary theory, seizes power. That is to say, he wins revolutionary power. What is Lenin's great merit? Lenin has the extraordinary merit of having made a thoroughgoing interpretation of Marx's thought, of having carried it into practice and having developed it under new circumstances, as is the case of a revolutionary party in power. That he developed an entire theory, thought of extraordinary depth, there is not the slightest doubt. That is Lenin's great historical merit as theoretician and leader.

Marxism is continuing to develop. Now, one has only to read Khrushchev's report to the 22nd Congress, which is a wholly political treatise, one that begins to confront an entirely new task, the building of communism. . . .

. . . We had to choose between remaining under the domination, under the exploitation and, furthermore, the insolence of imperialism, to go on putting up with Yankee ambassadors giving the orders here, keeping our country in the state of poverty it was in, or making an anti-imperialist revolution, making a socialist revolution.

There was no alternative. We chose the only honorable road, the only loyal road that we could follow for our country, and in keeping with the tradition of our revolutionary forefathers, in keeping with the tradition of all those who fought for the good of our country. That is the path we have followed: the path of anti-imperialist struggle, the path of the socialist Revolution. Moreover, there was no room for any other position. Any other position would have been a false position, an absurd position. We will never adopt such a position, nor will we ever waver. Never!

Imperialism should know well that, for all time, we will never have anything to do with it. And imperialism must know that however great our difficulties, however hard our struggle to build our country, to build the future of our country, to write a history worthy of our country, imperialism must not harbor the slightest hope so far as we are concerned.

Many who did not understand these things before understand them today. And they will understand them more and more. For all of us, these things become ever clearer, more evident, and more indisputable.

This is the path that the Revolution had to follow: the path of anti-imperialism and the path of socialism, that is, the path of nationalization of all the big industries, nationalization of big business, nationalization and social ownership of the basic means of production; a path of planned development of our economy at a pace that our resources permit, and that the aid we are receiving from abroad permits. Another truly favorable thing for our Revolution has been the fact that we have been able to count on the aid and solidarity which have enabled us to carry our Revolution forward without the enormous sacrifices that other peoples have had to make.

The Revolution had to be anti-imperialist and socialist. Good. There could have been only one anti-imperialist and socialist Revolution, because there is but one revolution. And that is the great dialectical truth of mankind: imperialism, and imperialism versus socialism. The result of this: the victory of socialism, the triumph of the epoch of socialism, the overcoming of the stage of capitalism and imperialism, the establishment of the era of socialism, and later on the era of communism.

No one need be scared by that; there won't be any communism—I'm saying this for any anti-communists left out there—there won't be any communism for at least thirty years.

Just so even our enemies will get to understand what Marxism is. In a nutshell, simply, remember that you just cannot skip over an entire historical stage. Perhaps, today, some underdeveloped countries can skip over the stage of building capitalism, that is, they can start developing the economy of a country through planning and along the path of socialism, but they cannot skip over the stage of socialism. The Soviet Union, itself, after forty years, is just beginning to build communism and hopes to have made considerable progress in this area at the end of twenty years. Thus, we are in a stage of the building of socialism.

What is the socialism we have to apply here? Utopian socialism? We simply have to apply scientific socialism. That is why I began by saying with complete frankness that we believe in Marxism, that we believe it is the most correct, the most scientific theory, the only truly revolutionary theory. I say that here with complete satisfaction (*applause*) and with complete confidence: I am a Marxist-Leninist, and I shall be a Marxist-Leninist to the end of my life (*prolonged applause*).

And what kind of a Marxist-Leninist am I? Am I a half-way one? We revolutionaries don't know how to be anything halfway. We only know how to be 100 per cent something. And to that we shall dedicate our efforts, our energies, our entire selves. Moreover, it is a great satisfaction to have been illiterate at the age of eighteen and to feel revolutionary as I do now at thirty odd years—I think the "odd years" run to thirty-six (*laughter and applause*). I've learned a thing or two in eighteen years, and still have a lot to learn! And that is what we are telling the people, with complete candor, with complete loyalty, with all clarity, as I have always spoken to the people, always with complete frankness.

Did I have prejudices? I believe it is good to talk about that. Did I have prejudices about the Communists? Yes. Was I ever influenced by imperialist and reactionary propaganda against the Communists? Yes. What did I think about the Communists? Did I think they were thieves? No, never; I always regarded the Communists—at the university and elsewhere—as honorable and honest people and all that. . . . But, well, that is no special merit, because almost everyone recognizes these qualities in them. Did I have the idea they were sectarian? Yes. Why did I have such opinions about the Communists? Simply, I am absolutely convinced that the ideas I had about the Communists—not about Marxism, nor about the Communist Party—like the ideas many people have, were the product of the propaganda and prejudices instilled in us since childhood, practically from school age, in the university, in the movies and everywhere else. I should say so. Do I believe they could make mistakes? Yes, I believe they can make mistakes. Marx, Engels and Lenin could make mistakes, and they themselves were the first to admit that they could be wrong, that they could err, because they did not think themselves infallible. . . .

A revolutionary party is a selective party which leads. It leads and works basically through its mass organizations, through labor unions, youth organizations, women's federations, defense committees (which, in this case, is an invention of the Cuban Revolution and is also a fantastic mass organization), peasant associations, cooperatives and the farms which are now in the unions. In other words, it leads and guides through all of these mass organizations.

Therefore, the standard that the political organization of the Cuban Revolution will have to follow will be, above all, the standard of selection and quality. It will not be a quantitative organization; it will be a qualitative organization.

We must say that as this is a product of the union of different revolutionary organizations, it is logical that in this initial stage the standard shouldn't be applied too rigidly, since one of the steps in the plan to organize this force—the integration of this revolutionary force—is to train revolutionary cadres. That is, in this initial stage of unification, we cannot logically set as strict requirements as they will have to be in the future, because all the comrades and cadres of the separate organizations have to be integrated into one organization and many of them are engaged in study and training.

This organization will be restricted in membership. It will not be small in number; it will be large, but not too large numerically, because we are going to be very demanding in our requirements for membership in the political organization of the Revolution. Furthermore, as we face greater demands, more conditions and more requirements will be laid down for membership in the United Party of the Socialist Revolution. We will establish a strict standard of selection for it is better to be selective before admitting, than to expel after admitting.

Because, moreover, the enthusiasm of the masses, the revolutionary spirit of the masses is so great, we know that a party which takes shape, develops, and grows strong under these conditions has the advantage of being able to recruit the best elements, the most positive elements from among the masses, and make them members of that organization. It is fundamental that precisely the best of the people, the best of the mass organizations should get the honor and at the same time, fulfill the honored role of membership in the United Party of the Socialist Revolution.

And the more this is so, the more every worker, every peasant, every intellectual, every citizen will appreciate it. It is necessary to point out that any citizen can become a member of the United Party of the Socialist Revolution, whether he is a worker or not. In other words, the doors are open to any true revolutionary who identifies with the Revolution and is willing to follow the standards set and to accept fully and with conviction the program of the United Party of the Socialist Revolution.

CHINA CHALLENGES RUSSIA

Beginning in 1960, the resistance of Communist China to Soviet leadership in the Communist movement led to an exchange of veiled criticisms and innuendos between the two Communist powers. In 1963 the Chinese brought the controversy into the open with a direct attack on the record of the Soviet leadership, to which the Russians replied in like manner. Using the same Marxist-Leninist doctrine against each other, Russia and China had brought international Communism to the verge of a split into two antagonistic movements.

LETTER OF THE COMMUNIST PARTY OF CHINA
TO THE COMMUNIST PARTY OF THE SOVIET UNION

It is the common and sacred duty of the Communist and Workers' parties of all countries to uphold and strengthen the unity of the international Communist movement. The Chinese and Soviet parties bear a heavier responsibility for the unity of the entire Socialist [i.e., Communist] camp and international Communist movement and should of course make commensurately greater efforts.

A number of major differences of principle now exist in the international Communist movement. But however serious these differences, we should exercise patience and find ways to eliminate them so that we can unite our forces and strengthen the struggle against our common enemy. . . .

The general line of the international Communist movement must take as its guiding principle the Marxist-Leninist revolutionary theory concerning the historical mission of the proletariat and must not depart from it.

The Moscow meetings of 1957 and 1960 adopted the Declaration and the Statement respectively after a full exchange of views and in accordance with the principle of reaching unanimity through consultation. The two documents point out the characteristics of our epoch and the

From the letter of the Central Committee of the Communist Party of China to the Central Committee of the Communist Party of the Soviet Union (reprinted in *The Peking Review,* June 16, 1963).

common laws of Socialist revolution and Socialist construction, and lay down the common line of all the Communist and Workers' parties. They are the common program of the international Communist movement.

It is true that for several years there have been differences within the international Communist movement in the understanding of and the attitude toward, the Declaration of 1957 and the Statement of 1960. The central issue here is whether or not to accept the revolutionary principles of the Declaration and the Statement. In the last analysis, it is a question of whether or not to accept the universal truth of Marxism-Leninism, whether or not to recognize the universal significance of the road of the October Revolution, whether or not to accept the fact that the people still living under the imperialist and capitalist system, who comprise two thirds of the world's population, need to make revolution, and whether or not to accept the fact that the people already on the Socialist road, who comprise one third of the world's population, need to carry their revolution forward to the end.

It has become an urgent and vital task of the international Communist movement resolutely to defend the revolutionary principles of the 1957 Declaration and the 1960 Statement.

Only by strictly following the revolutionary teachings of Marxism-Leninism and the general road of the October Revolution is it possible to have a correct understanding of the revolutionary principles of the Declaration and the Statement and a correct attitude toward them.

What are the revolutionary principles of the Declaration and the Statement? They may be summarized as follows:

Workers of all countries, unite; workers of the world, unite with the oppressed peoples and oppressed nations; oppose imperialism and reaction in all countries; strive for world peace, national liberation, people's democracy and Socialism; consolidate and expand the Socialist camp; bring the proletarian world revolution step by step to complete victory; and establish a new world without imperialism, without capitalism and without the exploitation of man by man.

This, in our view, is the general line of the international Communist movement at the present stage. . . .

All social revolutions in the various stages of the history of mankind are historically inevitable and are governed by objective laws independent of man's will. Moreover, history shows that there never was a revolution which was able to achieve victory without zigzags and sacrifices.

With Marxist-Leninist theory as the basis, the task of the proletarian party is to analyze the concrete historical conditions, put forward the correct strategy and tactics, and guide the masses in bypassing hidden reefs, avoiding unnecessary sacrifices and reaching the goal step by step. Is it possible to avoid sacrifices altogether? Such is not the case with the slave revolutions, the serf revolutions, the bourgeois revolutions, or the national revolutions; nor is it the case with proletarian revolutions. Even if the guiding line of the revolution is correct, it is impossible to have a sure guarantee against setbacks and sacrifices in the course of the revolution. So long as a correct line is adhered to, the revolution is bound to triumph in the end. To abandon revolution on the pretext of avoiding sacrifices is in reality to demand that the people should for ever remain slaves and endure infinite pain and sacrifice. . . .

The proletarian party must be flexible as well as highly principled, and on occasion it must make such compromises as are necessary in the interests of the revolution. But it must never abandon principled policies and the goal of revolution on the pretext of flexibility and of necessary compromises.

The proletarian party must lead the masses in waging struggles against the enemies, and it must know how to utilize the contradictions among those enemies. But the purpose of using these contradictions is to make it easier to attain the goal of the people's revolutionary struggles and not to liquidate these struggles.

Countless facts have proved that, wherever the dark rule of imperialism and reaction exists, the people who form over 90 per cent of the population will sooner or later rise in revolution.

If Communists isolate themselves from the revolutionary demands of the masses, they are bound to lose the confidence of the masses and will be tossed to the rear by the revolutionary current.

If the leading group in any party adopt a nonrevolutionary line and convert it into a reformist party, then Marxist-Leninists inside and outside the party will replace them and lead the people in making revolution. In another kind of situation, the bourgeois revolutionaries will come forward to lead the revolution and the party of the proletariat will forfeit its leadership of the revolution. When the reactionary bourgeoisie betray the revolution and suppress the people, an opportunist line will cause tragic and unnecessary losses to the Communists and the revolutionary masses.

If Communists slide down the path of opportunism, they will degenerate into bourgeois nationalists and become appendages of the imperialists and the reactionary bourgeoisie.

There are certain persons* who assert that they have made the greatest creative contributions to revolutionary theory since Lenin and that they alone are correct. But it is very dubious whether they have ever really given consideration to the extensive experience of the entire world communist movement, whether they have ever really considered the interests, the goal and tasks of the international proletarian movement as a whole, and whether they really have a general line for the international Communist movement which conforms with Marxism-Leninism.

In the last few years the international Communist movement and the national-liberation movement have had many

* I.e., Khrushchev and his supporters. [Ed.]

experiences and many lessons. There are experiences which people should praise and there are experiences which make people grieve. Communists and revolutionaries in all countries should ponder and seriously study these experiences of success and failure, so as to draw correct conclusions and useful lessons from them.

The Socialist [i.e., Communist] countries and the revolutionary struggles of the oppressed peoples and nations support and assist each other.

The national-liberation movements of Asia, Africa and Latin America and the revolutionary movements of the people in the capitalist countries are a strong support to the Socialist countries. It is completely wrong to deny this.

The only attitude for the Socialist countries to adopt towards the revolutionary struggles of the oppressed peoples and nations is one of warm sympathy and active support; they must not adopt a perfunctory attitude, or one of national selfishness or of great-power chauvinism.

Lenin said, "Alliance with the revolutionaries of the advanced countries and with all the oppressed peoples against any and all the imperialists—such is the external policy of the proletariat." Whoever fails to understand this point and considers that the support and aid given by the Socialist countries to the oppressed peoples and nations are a burden or charity is going counter to Marxism-Leninism and proletarian internationalism.

The superiority of the Socialist system and the achievements of the Socialist countries in construction play an exemplary role and are an inspiration to the oppressed peoples and the oppressed nations.

But this exemplary role and inspiration can never replace the revolutionary struggles of the oppressed peoples and nations. No oppressed people or nation can win liberation except through its own staunch revolutionary struggle.

Certain persons have onesidedly exaggerated the role of peaceful competition between Socialist and imperialist countries in their attempt to substitute peaceful competition for the revolutionary struggles of the oppressed peoples and nations. According to their preaching, it would seem

that imperialism will automatically collapse in the course
of this peaceful competition and that the only thing the
oppressed peoples and nations have to do is to wait quietly
for the advent of this day.

What does this have in common with Marxist-Leninist
views?

Moreover, certain persons have concocted the strange
tale that China and some other Socialist countries want
"to unleash wars" and to spread Socialism by "wars between states." As the Statement of 1960 points out, such
tales are nothing but imperialist and reactionary slanders.
To put it bluntly, the purpose of those who repeat these
slanders is to hide the fact they are opposed to revolutions
by the oppressed peoples and nations of the world and opposed to others supporting such revolutions. . . .

Every Socialist country must rely mainly on itself for its
construction.

In accordance with its own concrete conditions, every
Socialist country must rely first of all on the diligent labor
and talents of its own people, utilize all its available resources fully and in a planned way, and bring all its potential into play in Socialist construction. Only thus can it build
Socialism effectively and develop its economy speedily.

This is the only way for each Socialist country to
strengthen the might of the entire Socialist camp and en-
hance its capacity to assist the revolutionary cause of the
international proletariat. Therefore, to observe the principle
of mainly relying on oneself in construction is to apply
proletarian internationalism concretely.

If, proceeding only from its own partial interest, any
Socialist country unilaterally demands that other fraternal
countries submit to its needs, and uses the pretext of op-
posing what they call "going it alone" and "nationalism"
to prevent other fraternal countries from applying the
principle of relying mainly on their own efforts in their
construction and from developing their economies on the
basis of independence, or even goes to the length of putting

economic pressure on other fraternal countries—then these
are pure manifestations of national egoism. . . .

It is now more than ever necessary for all Communists
to unite on the basis of Marxism-Leninism and proletarian
internationalism and of the Declaration and the Statement
unanimously agreed upon by the fraternal parties.

Together with Marxist-Leninist parties and revolutionary
people the world over, the Communist party of China will
continue its unremitting efforts to uphold the interests of
the Socialist camp and the international Communist move-
men, the cause of the emancipation of the oppressed
peoples and nations, and the struggle against imperialism
and for world peace.

We hope that events which grieve those near and dear
to us and only gladden the enemy will not recur in the
international Communist movement in the future.

The Chinese Communists firmly believe that the Marxist-
Leninists, the proletariat and the revolutionary people everywhere will unite more closely, overcome all difficulties
and obstacles and win still greater victories in the struggle
against imperialism and for world peace, and in the fight
for the revolutionary cause of the people of the world and
the cause of international Communism.

Workers of all countries, unite! Workers and oppressed
peoples and nations of the world, unite! Oppose our common enemy!

PART ONE—MARXISM:

The most important books by Marx, apart from those represented in this volume, are the following: *Economic and Philosophical Manuscripts of 1844* (English translation, Moscow: Foreign Languages Publishing House, 1956); *The German Ideology* (1846; English translation, New York: International Publishers, 1947); *The Poverty of Philosophy* (1847; English translation, New York: International Publishers, n.d.); and *The Civil War in France* (1871; New York: International Publishers, 1940).

Engel's most important works, apart from the *Anti-Dühring*, include *The Condition of the Working Class in England* (1844; London: Allen and Unwin, 1926); *The Origin of the Family, Private Property, and the State* (1884; Moscow: FLPH, 1954); and *Ludwig Feuerbach and the End of Classical German Philosophy* (1888; Moscow: FLPH, 1950).

The basic collection of the works of Marx and Engels is the German "Historical and Critical Collected Edition of Marx and Engels" (*Marx-Engels Historisch-Kritische Gesamtausgabe*, Berlin: Dietz, 1927–   ), not yet complete. Most of Marx's important writings are contained in *Karl Marx: Selected Works* (2 vols., New York: International Publishers [1936–37]), and a different selection from both Marx and Engels is available in *Selected Works of Karl Marx and Friedrich Engels* (2 vols., Moscow: FLPH, 1958). Marx, *Capital and Other Writings* (New York: Modern Library, 1932) contains an abridgment of *Das Kapital;* it is not to be confused with the full first volume published as Marx, *Capital* (New York: Modern Library, n.d.). Briefer excerpts from a wide range of writings are available in Lewis S. Feuer, ed., *Marx and Engels: Basic Writings on Politics and Philosophy* (New York: Anchor Books, 1959), and in T. B. Bottomore and Maximilien Rubel, eds., *Karl Marx: Selected Writings in Sociology and Social Philosophy.*

The theory of Marxism is explained and evaluated in the following works: R. N. C. Hunt, *The Theory and Practice of Communism* (Baltimore: Penguin Books, 1963); Alfred G. Meyer, *Marxism—The Unity of Theory and Practice* (Cambridge, Mass.: Harvard University Press, 1954); and (for advanced students) George Lichtheim, *Marxism: An Historical and Critical Study* (New York: Praeger, 1961). See also my essays, "Fate and Will in the Marxian Philosophy of History," *Journal of the History of Ideas* (October 1960) and "Marxian Theories of Historical Dynamics," in Werner Cahnman and Alvin Boskoff, eds., *Sociology and History: Theory and Research* (New York: The Free Press of Glencoe, 1964). A good personal account of Marx and Engels is contained in Edmund Wilson, *To the Finland Station* (New York: Anchor Books, 1953). A basic reference is G. D. H. Cole, *A History of Socialist Thought* (5 vols. in 7 parts, London: Macmillan,

1953–1960). On "revisionism," see Peter Gay, *The Dilemma of Democratic Socialism* (New York: Collier Books, 1962).

PART TWO—RUSSIAN COMMUNISM:

Lenin's collected works have never been completely translated, though some important volumes were published by International Publishers (New York), and the Foreign Languages Publishing House in Moscow has brought out several volumes of a translation of the most recent Russian edition.

Trotsky's important books in translation include *Our Revolution* (1906; English translation, New York: Holt, 1918); *The First Five Years of the Communist International* (2 vols., New York: Pioneer Publishers, 1945, 1953); *The Permanent Revolution* (New York: Pioneer Publishers, 1931); and *The Revolution Betrayed* (New York: Doubleday, 1937).

Stalin's *Collected Works* (English translation, 13 vols., Moscow: FLPH, 1952–55) extend up to 1935. Selections of his most important articles and speeches have been translated in various editions entitled *Leninism* or *Problems of Leninism* (Moscow: FLPH).

Translations of Khrushchev's speeches were published in numerous Soviet volumes prior to his fall, as well as in the weekly *Current Digest of the Soviet Press* (New York). A good collection with critical commentary is Thomas P. Whitney, ed., *Khrushchev Speaks: Selected Speeches, Articles, and Press Conferences, 1949–1961* (Ann Arbor: University of Michigan Press, 1963). Khrushchev's career is described in Bertram D. Wolfe, *Khrushchev and Stalin's Ghost* (New York: Praeger, 1957), which includes the text of Khrushchev's famous "secret speech" denouncing Stalin in 1956.

Some general collections of excerpts from the writings of the Soviet leaders are Robert V. Daniels, *A Documentary History of Communism* (2 vols., New York: Vintage Books, 1962) and Robert H. McNeal, ed., *Lenin, Stalin, Khrushchev: Voices of Bolshevism* (Englewood Cliffs, New Jersey: Prentice-Hall, 1963).

There are many texts of Russian history that cover the background and development of Soviet Communism. Among the best are Jesse Clarkson, *A History of Russia* (New York: Random House, 1961), and Michael Florinsky, *Russia: A Short History* (New York: Macmillan, 1964). For a short survey with emphasis on Soviet Russia see Robert V. Daniels, *Russia* (Modern Nations in Historical Perspective series, Englewood Cliffs, New Jersey: Prentice-Hall, 1965). On the Russian revolutionary movement and the origin of the Bolshevik Party, see Avrahm Yarmolinsky, *Road to Revolution* (New York: Collier Books, 1962), Leopold Haimson, *The Russian Marxists and the Origins of Bolshevism* (Cambridge, Mass.: Harvard University Press, 1955), and Bertram Wolfe's triple biography of Lenin, Trotsky, and Stalin, *Three Who Made a Revolution* (New York: Dial, 1948). The best individual biographies are Louis Fischer, *The*

Life of Lenin (New York: Harper and Row, 1964), Isaac Deutscher, *Stalin: A Political Biography* (New York: Oxford, 1949), and Deutscher's three-volume work on Trotsky, *The Prophet Armed, The Prophet Unarmed,* and *The Prophet Outcast* (New York: Oxford, 1954, 1959, 1964).

The standard history of the Revolution of 1917 is William Henry Chamberlin, *The Russian Revolution* (2 vols., New York: Macmillan, 1935). It may be supplemented by Trotsky's *History of the Russian Revolution* (3 vols. in one, Ann Arbor: University of Michigan Press, 1957) and the documents in Robert P. Browder and Alexander Kerensky, eds., *The Russian Provisional Government, 1917* (Stanford, California: Stanford University Press, 1961). The Revolution and the first ten years of the Soviet regime are studied in detail in E. H. Carr, *A History of Soviet Russia* (7 vols. in 8 parts to date, New York: Macmillan, 1950–   ). The history of the Communist party from its origins to the present is recounted in Leonard Schapiro, *The Communist Party of the Soviet Union* (New York: Random House, 1960), while the official view may be found in Boris N. Ponomarev *et al.*, eds., *History of the CPSU* (Moscow: FLPH, 1960).

The evolution of Marxist theory in Soviet Russia is sketched in Klaus Mehnert, *Stalin vs. Marx* (London: Allen and Unwin, 1952), and analyzed in detail in Gustav Wetter, *Dialectical Materialism* (New York: Praeger, 1958); the official text is Otto V. Kuusinen, ed., *Fundamentals of Marxism-Leninism* (Moscow: FLPH, 1961). Other aspects of the Soviet system are well covered in Merle Fainsod, *How Russia is Ruled* (Cambridge, Mass.: Harvard University Press, rev. ed., 1963), Alec Nove, *The Soviet Economy: An Introduction* (New York: Praeger, 1961), and Kent Geiger and Alex Inkeles, eds., *Soviet Society: A Book of Readings* (Boston: Houghton-Mifflin, 1961). On recent developments see Myron Rush, *Political Succession in the USSR* (New York: Columbia University Press, 1965) and Leonard Schapiro, ed., *The USSR and the Future* (New York: Praeger, 1963), which contains the texts of all the Communist Party programs and commentaries on the new one.

PART THREE—VARIETIES OF COMMUNISM:

The Communist movement as a whole is described and analyzed in Alfred G. Meyer, *Communism* (New York: Random House, 1960), and in Robert V. Daniels, *The Nature of Communism* (New York: Vintage Books, 1963). A presentation written especially for high school students is Robert V. Daniels, *Understanding Communism* (Syracuse: Singer, 1964). The history of the movement is summarized in Massimo Salvadori, *The Rise of Modern Communism* (New York: Holt, rev. ed., 1963), and told in detail in Hugh Seton-Watson, *From Lenin to Khrushchev: The History of World Communism* (New York: Praeger, 1960). The motivations and weaknesses of the movement are explored in Gabriel Almond, *The Appeals of Communism*

(Princeton, New Jersey: Princeton University Press, 1954) and in Richard N. Crossman, ed., *The God that Failed* (New York: Harper, 1949).

There are numerous studies of Communism in particular countries and regions of the world, with the following representative items most recommended: Franz Borkenau, *European Communism* (New York: Harper, 1953); Irving Howe and Lewis Coser, *The American Communist Party: A Critical History (1919–1957)* (Boston: Beacon Press, 1957); Adam Ulam, *Titoism and the Cominform* (Cambridge, Mass.: Harvard University Press, 1952); Fred Warner Neal, *Titoism in Action: The Reforms in Yugoslavia After 1948* (Berkeley, California: University of California Press, 1958); Theodore Draper, *Castro's Revolution: Myths and Realities* (New York: Praeger, 1962); Malcolm Kennedy, *A History of Communism in East Asia* (New York: Praeger, 1957); and Robert C. North, *Moscow and Chinese Communists* (Stanford, California: Stanford University Press, 1953). For a brief background, see Kenneth Scott Latourette, *China* (Modern Nations in Historical Perspective series, Englewood Cliffs, New Jersey: Prentice-Hall, 1965), and Arthur A. Cohen, *The Communism of Mao Tse-tung* (Chicago: University of Chicago Press, 1964). For the writings of the Chinese leaders, see Conrad Brant, Benjamin Schwartz, and John K. Fairbank, eds., *A Documentary History of Chinese Communism* (Cambridge, Mass.: Harvard University Press, 1952), and Mao Tse-tung, *Collected Works* (New York: International Publishers, 1954). For a comparison of China and Russia, see Robert V. Daniels, "The Chinese Revolution in Russian Perspective," *World Politics* (January 1961). On Southeast Asia, see Bernard Fall, *The Two Viet Nams: A Political and Military Analysis* (New York: Praeger, 1963).

Relations between Soviet Russia and the non-Communist world are treated in many specialized works but few good general ones; some exceptions are George Kennan, *Russia and the West under Lenin and Stalin* (Boston: Atlantic–Little, Brown, 1960), and Alvin Z. Rubinstein, ed., *The Foreign Policy of the Soviet Union* (New York: Random House, 1960). For an interpretation of the role of theory in Soviet foreign policy, see Robert V. Daniels, "What the Russians Mean," *Commentary* (October 1962), reprinted in Norman Graebner, ed., *The Cold War* (Boston: Heath, 1964). Relations among the Communist countries and the Sino-Soviet schism are the subject of numerous good books, including Zbigniew Brzezinski, *The Soviet Bloc: Unity and Conflict* (New York: Praeger, 1961), and Edward Crankshaw, *The New Cold War: Moscow vs. Pekin* (Baltimore: Penguin Books, 1963). The chief documents of the schism are compiled in Alexander Dallin *et al.*, eds., *Diversity in International Communism* (New York: Columbia University Press, 1963).

To keep current on the Communist movement, there is no better source than the bimonthly journal of the United States Information Agency, *Problems of Communism*.

STUDIES IN POLITICAL SCIENCE

Original studies on vital topics in the field of government and politics, attractively bound in sturdy paper covers and priced from 95¢ to $1.95.